𝔗𝔥𝔢 𝔇𝔞𝔦𝔩𝔶 𝔗𝔢𝔩𝔢𝔤𝔯𝔞𝔭𝔥

Judith Keppel's Quiz Book

Judith Keppel

EBURY
PRESS

First published in the United Kingdom in 2001

13579108642

© 2001 Judith Keppel

First published by Ebury Press
Random House, 20 Vauxhall Bridge Road,
London SW1V 2SA

Random House Australia (Pty) Limited
20 Alfred Street, Milsons Point, Sydney,
New South Wales 2061, Australia

Random House New Zealand Limited
18 Poland Road, Glenfield, Auckland 10, New Zealand

Random House South Africa (Pty) Limited
Endulini, 5a Jubilee Road, Parktown 2193, South Africa

Random House Group Limited Reg. No. 954009

www.randomhouse.co.uk

A CIP catalogue record for this book is available from the British Library.

ISBN 0 09 188153 6

Typeset by anizdamani@aol.com

Printed and bound in Great Britain by Bookmarque Ltd, Croydon, Surrey

CONTENTS

INTRODUCTION

One of the questions people most often ask me is 'How did you feel when the million pound question came up?' (That question was: 'Who was Eleanor of Aquitaine married to? A: Henry I; B: Henry II; C: Richard I; D: John'). My first instinctive reaction was that it was Henry II, that I knew it. WOW! There was a split second when I felt absolutely certain.

But it was the calm before the mental storm. It is amazing how the possibility of blowing £468,000 can create doubt in your mind and a few moments later Doubt began to mutter about Henry I. So I knew that I had to slow down and make absolutely sure that my first feeling was right.

This is where Luck, the indispensable and elusive ingredient of all success, came in. I had had the good fortune to have driven home from a holiday through France that summer and had spent the night at a town called Fontevraud-L'Abbaye in the Loire valley. I had decided to stop there because there was a garden I wanted to see and I knew nothing about the Abbey. As it turned out the garden was disappointing but the Abbey was spectacular and, more importantly, it housed the tombs of several of the Plantagenet kings and the Queen Mother of the dynasty, Eleanor of Aquitaine. In the huge, otherwise empty church, she lay side by side with her husband and two of her sons, three of the four kings whose names were to come up on the screen in that fateful multiple choice answer in November. I had also had the luck to have 'done' Henry II for A Levels at school and, although that had been more years ago than I care to count, a few vague memories floated back. Despite all this, I was still not 100 per cent sure but more like about 85 per cent that I had got the Henrys right and I suppose this is where the 'What the hell?' gambling instinct came into play. I remember thinking that, having got that far, I had a kind of obligation to Fate to go the whole way and that at least I'd be an heroic loser if I got it wrong. With hindsight, that was pure insanity and I hope I never have such a thought again!

From that little tale, it is easy see that there were four elements that came into play in the process that led me to the jumping off point. The first, instinct; the second, caution; the third, luck; and the fourth, the willingness to take a risk. In general I believe in trusting my instinctive reactions. There is usually something in them that should not be ignored. But I never trust them blindly. They need checking out using a bit of logic and thought and memory and any other mental powers that can be dredged up. On the other hand, luck is luck and for the most part beyond control but it is of course linked with gambling. I am not normally a gambler, have never won a raffle, don't do the Lottery and I only bet on the Grand National, but I did feel that my luck was running with me that day. On the morning of the recording, I had found a crumpled £10 note in the street which I had felt to be a good omen and then when Eleanor of Aquitaine came up, I had a vivid picture in my mind of the tombs in the abbey church and an awareness that I had fallen on them almost accidentally.

So far as acquiring general knowledge at this sort of level is concerned, it is helpful to be curious and have a magpie mind. I am normally so vague I can't remember what day of the week it is and there is no way that I could ever explain anything seriously intellectual such as Einstein's Theory of Relativity. All I know about it is that it exists. Instead my head is stuffed with completely useless (until November 2000!) simple facts which stick in my mind for no good reason other than that they are in some way slightly quirky. Quirkiness is often fun or interesting, amusing or silly and in this book I hope you will find plenty of those sort of questions to divert you.

How to Use this Book

I have devised a very simple game that can be played with two or more contestants and a quiz master. The number of rounds should be determined beforehand – I suggest ten but it could be more or fewer. Each contestant answers a question in turn. The questions have been divided into four levels of difficulty and the first question must be an 'Easy' one. After that the contestant can choose his level. The harder the question, the more points are won for each correct answer.

One point for 'Easy'
Two points for 'Tricky'
Three points for 'Hard'
Four for 'Very Difficult'

At the 'Very Difficult' level, the contestant can 'Take a Hint from Judith' once he has heard the question but, if he gets it right, he will only score two points instead of a possible four. These hints are based on the fifth element that can determine success in multiple choice quizzes – deduction. If you can narrow it down to two possibilities, it might just be worth a guess.

Hint – Play tactically! Go for the points early on and if you're successful, everyone else will have to go for the difficult ones as well or they'll have no chance of catching up.

Be brave! Have fun – it's only a game!

Acknowledgements

I'd like to thank Martin Smith, Roger Highfield, Sinclair McKay and Susannah Charlton from the *Daily Telegraph* for all their invaluable help with this book. I am also indebted to my old friend Priscilla Williams for many helpful suggestions and above all to Mary Killen, who put me on my path as a quiz setter for the *Daily Telegraph* in the first place.

Section 1:

Easy

Which actress played the part of Evita in the film of the same name? 1

A Gwynneth Paltrow

Elaine Paige B

C Madonna

Julia Roberts D

Which model of the Earth's outer layer views it as one in which the pieces are constantly moving in relation to each other? 2

A Bucket tectonics

Pan tectonics B

C Plate tectonics

Saucer tectonics D

What was the name of the ship in which the Pilgrim Fathers set sail for America? 3

A Marie Celeste

Mayflower B

C Queen Mary

Mary Rose D

Which saint became identified with Father Christmas? 4

A St Nicholas

St Thomas B

C St Stephen

St Michael D

5 In which club in Liverpool were the Beatles discovered?

A The Grotto

The Cavern B

C The Tunnel

The Black Hole D

6 Myxomatosis is a disease affecting which creatures?

A Deer

Horses B

C Cows

Rabbits D

7 In Norse mythology Thor was the god of which of the following?

A Hunting

Thunder B

C The Sea

War D

8 Which of the following trees is evergreen?

A Yew

Beech B

C Oak

Elm D

Who was known as the
Maid of Orleans?

9

A   Heloise

Josephine Bonaparte   B

C   Jeanne d'Arc

Jeanne Poisson   D

Which of the following drinks
contains the most caffeine per
fluid ounce?

10

A   Coffee

Tea   B

C   Coca-Cola

Lager   D

Insomnia is another name
for which problem?

11

A   Sleepwalking

Loss of appetite   B

C   Sleeplessness

Thirst   D

What frightened Miss Muffet
away from her tuffet?

12

A   Cow

Bumble bee   B

C   Spider

Buzzard   D

13 Which kind of animal can live the longest?

A	Man	
	Elephant	B
C	Tortoise	
	Parrot	D

14 The musical *West Side Story* was based on which Shakespeare play?

A	*Much Ado About Nothing*	
	Love's Labours Lost	B
C	*Romeo and Juliet*	
	The Tempest	D

15 Le Corbusier was associated with which field of the arts?

A	Architecture	
	Sculpture	B
C	Photography	
	Painting	D

16 Which British artist was celebrated for his paintings of horses?

A	Constable	
	Stubbs	B
C	Landseer	
	Sickert	D

Which mammal gives birth to the largest baby? 17

A   Elephant

Whale   B

C   Rhinoceros

Hippopotamus   D

Which king ordered the waves to turn back? 18

A   Ethelred the Unready

Canute   B

C   William the Conqueror

William IV   D

In 'Peter Pan' what was the name of the Darling family's dog? 19

A   Mama

Dada   B

C   Nana

Gaga   D

Which bird shares its name with an architect? 20

A   Lark

Wren   B

C   Robin

Eagle   D

21 On which river is the city of Washington, USA situated?

A St Lawrence

Potomac B

C Hudson

Mississippi D

22 Which disease affecting dogs is also a kind of paint?

A Whitewash

Distemper B

C Tempera

Gouache D

23 In a theatre, what is the area where the orchestra usually sits called?

A Stalls

Pit B

C Gallery

Circle D

24 At Halloween which vegetable is carved into a face and lit with a candle?

A Potato

Parsnip B

C Pumpkin

Marrow D

What is the term for cutting short the tail of a horse or a dog? 25

A Hocking

Blocking B

C Docking

Mocking D

Which is the southernmost tip of land in South Africa? 26

A Cape of Good Hope

Cape Horn B

C Cape Saint Vincent

Cape Farewell D

What is a joule? 27

A A unit of energy

A type of diamond B

C An instrument

A garden D

What is the name of the cat who chases after Jerry? 28

A Ben

Meg B

C Tom

Don D

29 Who is the patron saint of travellers?

A — St Nicholas

St George — B

C — St Christopher

St Andrew — D

30 The Tarot is a pack of cards used for what purpose?

A — Poker

Darts — B

C — Card houses

Fortune telling — D

31 Who first developed the political and economic system that became known as Communism?

A — Lenin

Stalin — B

C — Marx

Trotsky — D

32 In Greek mythology, where was the home of the gods?

A — Arcadia

Valhalla — B

C — Olympus

Hades — D

What nationality was Jules Rimet, who founded football's World Cup? 33

A Belgian

Swiss B

C French

Dutch D

What does it mean to reboot a computer? 34

A Restart it

Move it B

C Decorate it

Turn it off D

Sugar is classed in which category of food? 35

A Protein

Fat B

C Carbohydrate

Fibre D

Figures from dance halls, brothels and cafes in Montmartre were a favourite subject of which French painter? 36

A Degas

Toulouse Lautrec B

C Braque

Daumier D

37 The play *Hay Fever* was written by which dramatist?

A — John Osborne

Noel Coward — **B**

C — Oscar Wilde

Terence Rattigan — **D**

38 In which city is the Parthenon to be found?

A — Rome

London — **B**

C — Athens

Cairo — **D**

39 Whose unmade bed was recently exhibited as a work of art?

A — Robbie Williams

Tracy Emin — **B**

C — George Best

Posh and Becks — **D**

40 Insulin is commonly used to treat which disease?

A — Angina

Bronchitis — **B**

C — Chicken pox

Diabetes — **D**

On which island in the
Mediterranean is the Barbary
Ape found in the wild?

41

A — Malta

Gibraltar — **B**

C — Cyprus

Corfu — **D**

By which means is the age of
a tree calculated?

42

A — Measuring height

Measuring girth — **B**

C — Counting rings

Counting leaves — **D**

In the Old Testament,
which baby was found in
the bullrushes?

43

A — Jacob

Moses — **B**

C — Abraham

Isaac — **D**

What were the Celtic priests
of Ancient Britain known as?

44

A — Druids

Picts — **B**

C — Icenis

Zealots — **D**

45 Which of the following signs of the Zodiac is not symbolised by a real animal?

A Leo

Sagittarius B

C Taurus

Cancer D

46 In Wordsworth's opinion, what on 'Earth has not anything to show more fair'?

A The view from Westminster Bridge

A Daffodil B

C A rainbow

A perfect woman D

47 In golf, what do you call a score of three under par at a hole?

A Seagull

Birdie B

C Osprey

Albatross D

48 Johann Strauss was celebrated for which particular compositions?

A Lieder

Symphonies B

C Waltzes

Madrigals D

E A S Y

What is the name of the river which divides England from Scotland? 49

A Tay

Dee B

C Tweed

Tyne D

Kimberley, South Africa, is a production centre for which mineral? 50

A Tin

Iron B

C Gold

Silver D

In 1942, which island was awarded the George Cross for gallantry? 51

A Majorca

Malta B

C Ascension

Guernsey D

Which of the following is not one of Wales' national symbols? 52

A Leek

Primrose B

C Daffodil

Red Dragon D

53 As the crow flies, how many miles are there between Land's End and John o' Groats?

A — 806

535 — B

C — 603

926 — D

54 In ballet, a 'pas de deux' is danced by whom?

A — Corps de ballet

Soloist — B

C — Two dancers

Four dancers — D

55 Which of these breeds of cats has blue eyes?

A — Burmese

Siamese — B

C — Russian Blue

Abyssinian — D

56 Where in the world are the Everglades to be found?

A — Northern Territory, Australia

North Island, New Zealand — B

C — South Florida, USA

British Columbia, Canada — D

57 'Dr Livingstone, I presume' was the greeting of which explorer at the great encounter?

A Speke

B Burton

C Stanley

D Rhodes

58 Who won the Battle of Hastings in 1066?

A Wainwright the Wastrel

B Charles the Conqueror

C William the Conqueror

D Wallace the Warrior

59 Since 1946 Alistair Cooke has been sending which regular despatch from abroad?

A Letter from America

B Cable from Canada

C Notes from New Zealand

D Missive from Moscow

60 *Summoned by Bells* is the autobiography in verse of which poet?

A John Betjeman

B Ted Hughes

C Philip Larkin

D Alfred Tennyson

61 Who or what is Slieve Donard?

A Peak in Northern Ireland

Plant **B**

C Novelist

Racehorse **D**

62 The Grand Banks are associated with which industry?

A Financial Services

Gambling **B**

C Fishing

Mining **D**

63 Which is the largest desert in the world?

A Sahara

Kara Kum **B**

C Gobi

Australian Desert **D**

64 Which of these is not one of the Seven Deadly Sins?

A Anger

Greed **B**

C Sloth

Pessimism **D**

65 Under which kind of tree did the Buddha receive enlightenment?

A Banyan

B Bo

C Bay

D Blue cedar

66 Achilles was vulnerable in which part of his body?

A Hand

B Elbow

C Knee

D Heel

67 Sheryl Crow was a member of whose backing group before going solo?

A Janet Jackson

B Michael Jackson

C Germain Jackson

D Latoyah Jackson

68 What is the name of the Prime Minister's official country house?

A Draughts

B Marbles

C Chequers

D Halma

69 Which of these islands is not one of the Channel Islands?

A — Guernsey

Jersey — B

C — Cardigan

Sark — D

70 The English National Opera (ENO) is based at which London theatre?

A — Drury Lane

Barbican — B

C — Covent Garden

Coliseum — D

71 Hotlips Hoolihan was a character from which TV series?

A — *ER*

MASH — B

C — *NYPD*

Hawaii Five-0 — D

72 What was the name of the first President of the United States of America?

A — Thomas Jefferson

Abraham Lincoln — B

C — George Washington

Andrew Jackson — D

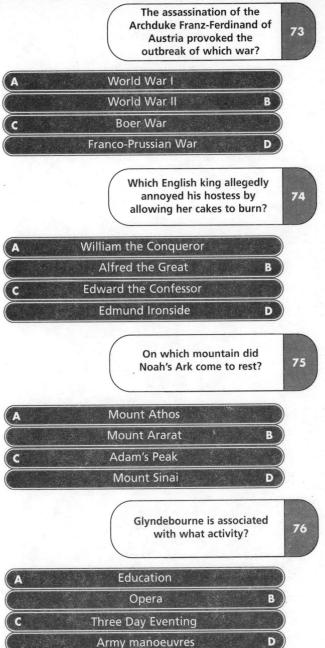

The assassination of the Archduke Franz-Ferdinand of Austria provoked the outbreak of which war? 73

A World War I

World War II B

C Boer War

Franco-Prussian War D

Which English king allegedly annoyed his hostess by allowing her cakes to burn? 74

A William the Conqueror

Alfred the Great B

C Edward the Confessor

Edmund Ironside D

On which mountain did Noah's Ark come to rest? 75

A Mount Athos

Mount Ararat B

C Adam's Peak

Mount Sinai D

Glyndebourne is associated with what activity? 76

A Education

Opera B

C Three Day Eventing

Army manoeuvres D

77 Who was defeated at the Battle of Waterloo?

A Wellington

Napoleon B

C Bismarck

The Tsar of Russia D

78 What is a snapdragon?

A Flower

Insect B

C Lizard

Fish D

79 What was the name of the ship in which Captain Cook first sailed to Australia?

A Beagle

Mary Rose B

C Endeavour

Resolution D

80 What do the initials RADA stand for?

A Royal Academy of Dancing Angels

Royal Academy of Design in Adverts B

C Royal Academy of Dramatic Arts

Royal Academy of Decorative Aims D

What were the Royalist supporters known as in the English Civil War? 81

A Roundheads

Cavaliers B

C Musketeers

Hussars D

In which city was President Kennedy assassinated? 82

A Des Moines

Denver B

C Dallas

Detroit D

Who invented the decibel, a unit of sound loudness? 83

A Alexander Graham Bell

Bel Mooney B

C Bel Air

Bel Canto D

Who lived in the Hundred Acre Wood? 84

A Mole and Ratty

Pooh and Piglet B

C The Flopsy Bunnies

The Little Grey Men D

85 What shirt number did Pele wear?

A One

B Six

C Eight

D Ten

86 William the Conqueror was the Duke of which French region?

A Aquitaine

B Provence

C Normandy

D Champagne

87 *The Moon's a Balloon* is the autobiography of which film actor?

A James Mason

B David Niven

C Erroll Flynn

D James Stewart

88 As he lay dying on the deck of the Victory, who did Nelson allegedly ask to kiss him?

A Emma Hamilton

B Hardy

C Florence Nightingale

D A Powder Monkey

Which Lord Mayor of London's only friend was once a cat? 89

A Ken Livingstone

Sir Robert Geffreye B

C Sir Richard Whittington

Samuel Pepys D

General Pinochet was president of which country? 90

A Peru

Ecuador B

C Colombia

Chile D

What do the initials AD stand for? 91

A After Domesday

Anno Domini B

C After Death

Ad Diem D

Which country is the world's largest producer of rubber? 92

A Sri Lanka

Brazil B

C Malaysia

India D

93 What is 'magma'?

A Plaque on teeth

Molten rock B

C Pondweed

Fishing bait D

94 Chernobyl, the site of a nuclear accident in 1986, is in which country?

A Iran

Mongolia B

C Ukraine

Lithuania D

95 A tornado is also known as which of the following?

A Whirligig

Twister B

C Spiraller

Wriggler D

96 In 1521, Martin Luther was excommunicated by which authority?

A The Feast of Katz

The Regime of Dhoggs B

C The Diet of Worms

The Dance of Burdes D

What is the name given to the British overseas touring rugby union side? **97**

A Cubs

Lions B

C Springboks

Wasps D

Which range of hills is known as the backbone of England? **98**

A Mendips

Cheviots B

C Pennines

Malverns D

Who did Flora Macdonald help to escape from Scotland after his defeat in battle? **99**

A Bonnie Prince Charlie

The Old Pretender B

C William Wallace

Robert the Bruce D

In which year was the present Queen crowned? **100**

A 1948

1950 B

C 1953

1956 D

101 By what name are card games played by one person known?

A Perseverance

Patience B

C Endurance

Ennui D

102 Which actor won an Oscar for his role in the film *Gladiator*?

A Tom Cruise

Charlton Heston B

C Russell Crowe

Tony Curtis D

103 Red currant jelly is often served with which meat?

A Beef

Lamb B

C Pork

Ham D

104 Coca-Cola originated from which country?

A Australia

Germany B

C USA

Mexico D

What sort of furniture is an ottoman? `105`

A	Seat
	Bed **B**
C	Table
	Cupboard **D**

Which French couturier introduced the 'New Look' after the Second World War? `106`

A	Yves St Laurent
	Christian Dior **B**
C	Hubert de Givenchy
	Balenciaga **D**

Chianti is a wine produced in which country? `107`

A	France
	Australia **B**
C	California
	Italy **D**

Marie Lloyd was celebrated in which branch of show business? `108`

A	Music Hall
	Concerts **B**
C	Circus
	Television **D**

109 With what is the game of Tiddlywinks played?

A   Dice

Counters   B

C   Sticks

Stones   D

110 In the Bible, what was the name of the giant killed by David?

A   Titan

Grim   B

C   Gog

Goliath   D

111 If you ordered 'petit pois' from a menu, what would you get?

A   Broad beans

Green beans   B

C   New potatoes

Peas   D

112 In World War II which German military leader in command of the Afrika Korps was known as the 'Desert Fox'?

A   Goering

Ludendorff   B

C   Keitel

Rommel   D

**'Their's not to reason why,
/ Their's but to do or die.'
To what did these lines refer?**

113

A   The Charge of the Light Brigade

The massacre at Glencoe   B

C   The Battle of Borodino

The Retreat from Moscow   D

**Which Roman Emperor first
invaded England?**

114

A   Caesar Augustus

Julius Caesar   B

C   Hadrian

Claudius   D

**Which Russian president
was associated with the
policies of 'glasnost' and
'perestroika'?**

115

A   Stalin

Kruschev   B

C   Gorbachev

Yeltsin   D

**What is the 'Naked Chef's'
real name?**

116

A   Clarissa Dickson Wright

Nik Rhodes   B

C   Jamie Oliver

Mrs Beaton   D

117 Naomi Campbell is well known in what capacity?

A Swimmer

Tennis Champion B

C Supermodel

Singer D

118 What is the name for a painting which depicts objects such as fruit or flowers?

A Low life

High Life B

C Still Life

Country Life D

119 Imelda Marcos was renowned for her collection of which items of clothing?

A Furs

Shoes B

C Hats

Bikinis D

120 Which pudding traditionally accompanies roast beef?

A Suet

Christmas B

C Yorkshire

Pease D

What was the name of Harry Potter's owl? 121

A Armwig

Hedwig B

C Toewig

D Legwig D

'Who dares wins' is the motto of which service? 122

A SAS

RAF B

C Royal Marines

Royal Navy D

In Kipling's *Jungle Book*, what was the name of the tiger? 123

A Bagheera

Baloo B

C Rikki Tikki Tavi

Shere Khan D

Who scored a hat-trick when England won the World Cup in 1966? 124

A Bobby Charlton

Bobby Moore B

C Geoff Hurst

Jimmy Greaves D

125 Which ocean current warms the coast of Britain?

A El Nino

Humboldt B

C Kuroshio

Gulf Stream D

126 Which of the *Little Women* died tragically of scarlet fever?

A Meg

Jo B

C Beth

Amy D

127 What is the name of the Scarlet Pimpernel?

A Sir Percy Blakeney

Richard Hannay B

C D'Artagnon

Guy Crouchback D

128 What is the Hobbit's real name?

A Frodo

Gollum B

C Gandalf

Bilbo Baggins D

129 Which American playwright was married to Marilyn Monroe?

A Tennessee Williams

B Arthur Miller

C Eugene O'Neill

D Clifford Odets

130 Where did Holly Golightly want to have breakfast?

A Bloomingdales

B Tiffany's

C Henri Bendel

D Starbucks

131 The title of the Jules Verne novel refers to how many leagues under the sea?

A Ten thousand

B Twenty thousand

C Thirty thousand

D Forty thousand

132 In Shakespeare's play, The *Taming of the Shrew* what is the shrew's name?

A Miranda

B Perdita

C Katherina

D Goneril

133 On which lake is the city of Chicago situated?

A Erie

Huron **B**

C Michigan °

Superior **D**

134 Which language would Jesus have spoken ?

A Hebrew

Aramaic **B**

C Arabic

Yiddish **D**

135 In the *Peanuts* cartoon what is the name of the bird?

A Snoopy

Linus **B**

C Woodstock

Schroeder **D**

136 The painters Monet, Manet, Renoir, Pisarro, Sisley belonged to which artistic movement?

A Cubism

Romanticism **B**

C Impressionism

Expressionism **D**

137 Who or what is the 'Old Lady of Threadneedle Street'?

A	The Bank of England	
	Margaret Thatcher	**B**
C	The Mansion House	
	Queen Victoria	**D**

138 In *Strewelpeter* which little boy refused to eat his soup?

A	Johnny	
	Augustus	**B**
C	Frederick	
	Peter	**D**

139 In Edward Lear's poem, what did the Pobble lack?

A	Ears	
	Eyes	**B**
C	Thumbs	
	Toes	**D**

140 On which part of a building would a gargoyle be found?

A	Floor	
	Ceiling	**B**
C	Roof	
	Foundation	**D**

141 The Jaberwocky is the invention of which writer?

A	Hilaire Belloc
	Lewis Carroll **B**
C	Edward Lear
	J R R Tolkien **D**

142 In the poem 'The Ancient Mariner', what is fatally shot?

A	The Wedding Guest
	The Pilot **B**
C	The Hermit
	The Albatross **D**

143 In Greek mythology, who carries the world on his shoulders?

A	Heracles
	Zeus **B**
C	Atlas
	Poseidon **D**

144 Whose diary was entitled *The Naked Civil Servant*?

A	Anthony Trollope
	Albert Speer **B**
C	Charles Dickens
	Quentin Crisp **D**

What does a laser generate? 145

A Water jet

Light B

C Supermarket labels

Bar codes D

What do sailors do when they splice the mainbrace? 146

A Climb the mast

Get hit by the boom B

C Have a drink

Go ashore D

At which Olympic Games did Mark Spitz win seven gold medals for swimming? 147

A 1968

1972 B

C 1976

1980 D

Poet's Corner is to be found in which London building? 148

A St Paul's Cathedral

Westminster Abbey B

C Highgate Cemetery

St Martin's-in-the-Fields D

149 By what name is the new modern art gallery opened in London in 2000 known?

A   Tate Britain

Tate Modern   **B**

C   The Dome

The London Eye   **D**

150 Which of these trees bears poisonous nuts?

A   Hazel

Horse Chestnut   **B**

C   Walnut

Sweet Chestnut   **D**

151 What was the name of Wendy's family in Peter Pan?

A   Sweeting

Truelove   **B**

C   Darling

Valentine   **D**

152 Which north-eastern English football club have recently changed their nickname from the Rokermen to the Black Cats?

A   Sunderland

Newcastle   **B**

C   Lincoln

Grimsby   **D**

'Buttons' appears in which Christmas pantomime? 153

A	Aladdin
B	Cinderella
C	Mother Goose
D	Robin Hood

Who wrote the novel *The Naked and the Dead*? 154

A	Nicholas Monserrat
B	Harold Robbins
C	John Steinbeck
D	Norman Mailer

Which feminist writer wrote *The Female Eunuch*? 155

A	Betty Friedan
B	Helen Gurley Brown
C	Marilyn French
D	Germaine Greer

With which athletic event do you associate the Fosbury Flop? 156

A	Steeplechase
B	Pole Vault
C	High Jump
D	Long Jump

157 In 1960, which novel was the subject of an obscenity trial?

A *Tropic of Cancer*

B *Love in the Time of Cholera*

C *Ulysses*

D *Lady Chatterley's Lover*

158 Rum and Coke are the main ingredients of which cocktail?

A Gimlet

B Harvey Wallbanger

C Cuba Libre

D Pina-Colada

159 For which team did Michael Schumacher drive when he won the Formula One world title in 2000?

A Benetton

B McLaren

C Ferrari

D Jordan

160 Which festival are children celebrating when they go 'Trick or Treating'?

A Guy Fawkes Night

B Christmas Eve

C Hallow'een

D Midsummer's Eve

EASY

What is on the reverse side of a two pence piece? **161**

A Dragon

Three Leopards B

C Thistle

Prince of Wales feathers D

Which royal residence was badly damaged by fire in the early 1990s? **162**

A Windsor

Balmoral B

C Sandringham

Buckingham Palace D

Anita Roddick was the founder of which chain of shops? **163**

A Tesco

Next B

C Oasis

The Body Shop D

'Too many cooks spoil the ...' Which of the following completes this proverb? **164**

A Bread

Broth B

C Butter

Beef D

165 Which was Harry Potter's house at school?

A	Gryffindor
	Ravenclaw **B**
C	Hufflepuff
	Slytherin **D**

166 What is the name of the monkey in the Babar books?

A	Breeze
	Zephyr **B**
C	Gale
	Tornado **D**

167 Jacqueline du Pre played which instrument?

A	Violin
	Piano **B**
C	Clarinet
	Cello **D**

168 Waterlilies were a favourite subject of which painter?

A	Constable
	Turner **B**
C	Monet
	Renoir **D**

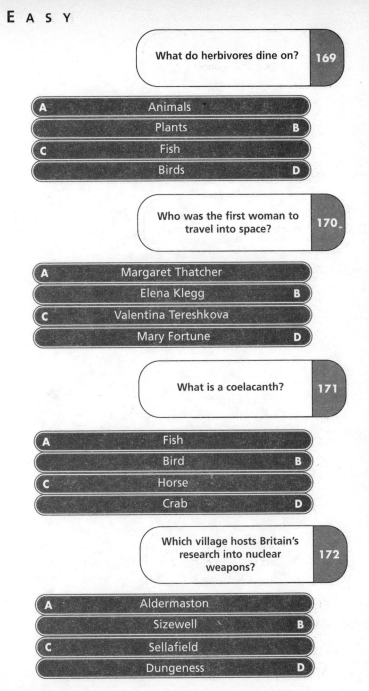

What do herbivores dine on? 169

A Animals

Plants B

C Fish

Birds D

Who was the first woman to travel into space? 170

A Margaret Thatcher

Elena Klegg B

C Valentina Tereshkova

Mary Fortune D

What is a coelacanth? 171

A Fish

Bird B

C Horse

Crab D

Which village hosts Britain's research into nuclear weapons? 172

A Aldermaston

Sizewell B

C Sellafield

Dungeness D

173 Which painter cut off his own ear?

A Rembrandt

El Greco B

C Van Gogh

Damien Hirst D

174 What is an integrated circuit also called?

A Potato

Wedge B

C Crisp

Chip D

175 Michaelangelo's sculpture of David is to be found in which city?

A Naples

Rome B

C Venice

Florence D

176 What modern invention is John Logie Baird famous for?

A Television

Holograms B

C CDs

DVDs D

In the 1960s, Jean Shrimpton was the muse of which photographer?

177

A   Cecil Beaton

David Bailey   B

C   Terence Donovan

Richard Avedon   D

What is the slang term for the complete malfunction of a computer?

178

A   Smash

Hash   B

C   Crash

Mash   D

Which of the following is an alloy?

179

A   Copper

Tin   B

C   Bronze

Silver   D

Who famously cried out 'Eureka' while he was having a bath?

180

A   Archimedes

Leonardo da Vinci   B

C   Peter Plumber

Lord Leverhulme   D

181 Which planet is closest to the Sun?

A Earth

Mars B

C Jupiter

Mercury D

182 What does a Geiger counter do?

A Counts Geigers

Measures radioactivity B

C Measures air pressure

Measures clicking D

183 James Boswell was the biographer of which of these literary men?

A Walter Scott

Lord Macauley B

C Samuel Johnson

Lord Byron D

184 What is the most plentiful element in the universe?

A Carbon

Uranium B

C Oxygen

Hydrogen D

What is a Noble gas? `185`

A	One of impeccable pedigree
	One discovered by a prince **B**
C	One that is mostly inert
	A gas with attitude **D**

In the Old Testament, what was the name of the 'Promised Land' of the Israelites? `186`

A	Sumeria
	Assyria **B**
C	Canaan
	Syria **D**

Which organisms causes Bubonic Plague? `187`

A	Fungi
	Bacteria **B**
C	Viruses
	Amoebas **D**

Whose famous diary opens on 1 January 1660? `188`

A	John Evelyn
	Kilvert **B**
C	Samuel Pepys
	Chips Channon **D**

189 'Rain, Steam and Speed' is the title of a painting by which artist?

A   Turner

Constable   B

C   L S Lowry

David Hockney   D

190 What covers more than 70 per cent of the Earth's surface?

A   Sea

Sand   B

C   Shells

Flies   D

191 What would you do with a Haiku?

A   Eat it

Wear it   B

C   Walk on it

Read it   D

192 In which cathedral is T S Eliot's *Murder in the Cathedral* set?

A   St Paul's

Durham   B

C   Lincoln

Canterbury   D

After Clare Francis ended her sailing career, she achieved success in what capacity?

193

A	Cook
Actress	B
C	Novelist
Sculptress	D

Which successful jockey later became a best-selling author?

194

A	Lester Piggott
Gordon Richards	B
C	Dick Francis
Terry Biddlecombe	D

What are diamonds made of?

195

A	Carbon
Silicon	B
C	Glass
Plastic	D

What does a person look like if described as 'peaky'

196

A	Tall
Angular	B
C	Ill
Short-sighted	D

197 What is a galaxy?

A   A star

A collection of stars   B

C   A planet

An asteroid   D

198 What causes the common cold?

A   Fungi

Bacteria   B

C   Viruses

Amoebas   D

199 Where is the hardest part of your body?

A   Heart

Head   B

C   Skin

Teeth   D

200 By which process do plants use energy from sunlight?

A   Picturesynthesis

Photosynthesis   B

C   Snapsynthesis

Slidesynthesis   D

In which TV soap did Anna Friel make her name?

201

A	*Eastenders*
	Brookside B
C	*Hollyoaks*
	Neighbours D

Which was Guy Ritchie's follow up film to *Lock, Stock and Two Smoking Barrels*?

202

A	*Grab*
	Snatch B
C	*Pinch*
	Heist D

Which actress plays the part of Mel in *Eastenders*?

203

A	Lucy Benjamin
	Letitia Dean B
C	Tamzin Outhwaite
	Natalie Cassidy D

What is the coloured part of an eye called?

204

A	Iris
	Rose B
C	Lily
	Crocus D

205 Michael Jackson's hit, 'Billie Jean', can be found on which album?

A *Bad*

Thriller B

C *Dangerous*

Blood on the Dance Floor D

206 Which artist had a greatest hits album called the *Immaculate Collection*?

A Eurythmics

Michael Jackson B

C Madonna

Elvis Presley D

207 Which of the following is a computer game character?

A Baron Bombem

Duke Nukem B

C Count Killem

Lord Losem D

208 Who played the part of Scarlet in the film *Gone With The Wind*?

A Merle Oberon

Vivien Leigh B

C Joan Fontaine

Joan Crawford D

209 Andrew Ridgeley and George Michael were the original member of which group?

A Duran Duran

Blur B

C Wham!

Take That D

210 What kind of bird is a kestrel?

A Owl

Falcon B

C Penguin

Thrush D

211 Which of these is not one of the Teletubbies?

A Tinky Winky

Po B

C Dipsy

Tipsy D

212 What was the name of Spice Girl Mel C's first single?

A 'Going up'

'Going down' B

C 'Coming in'

'Coming out' D

213 What is the name of the dog in the TV cartoon series *The Rugrats*?

A Rover

Spot B

C Spike

Jimmy D

214 What is the name of the fault line which runs the length of California?

A San Andreas

San Antonio B

C San Francisco

San Diego D

215 What is the name of Popeye's arch enemy?

A Olive Oyle

Captain Pugwash B

C Captain Birdseye

Bluto D

216 Buzz Lightyear was a character in which film?

A *Star Wars*

Superman B

C *Toy Story*

Close Encounters of the Third Kind D

Which actress played the title role in the 1960s film *Cleopatra*? `217`

A Joan Crawford

Elizabeth Taylor **B**

C Jane Russell

Jane Fonda **D**

Which football club shares Selhurst Park with Wimbledon? `218`

A Fulham

Crystal Palace **B**

C Chelsea

Brighton **D**

Which Russian composer wrote the score for the ballet *Swan Lake*? `219`

A Rimsky-Korsakov

Borodin **B**

C Tchaikovsky

Mussorgski **D**

Who invented the hovercraft? `220`

A David Flymo

Christopher Cockerell **B**

C James Dyson

Peter J Hoover **D**

221 Which dancer was accidentally strangled when her scarf got caught in the wheels of her car?

A Martha Graham

Josephine Baker B

C Beryl Grey

Isadora Duncan D

222 What was the name of the legendary outlaw who took from the rich and gave to the poor in the reign of bad King John?

A Allan-a-Dale

Will-o'-the-Wisp B

C Ned Kelly

Robin Hood D

223 Which tenor made the aria 'Nessun dorma' the soccer World Cup 1990 anthem in Rome?

A Gigli

Luciano Pavarotti B

C Jose Carreras

Willard White D

224 Blue Mountain coffee comes from which country?

A Jamaica

Brazil B

C Kenya

Java D

Who was said to be Hitler's favourite composer `225`

A	Mozart
	Beethoven **B**
C	Wagner
	Brahms **D**

Which singing voice is the lowest? `226`

A	Tenor
	Baritone **B**
C	Bass
	Counter-tenor **D**

Which of the following countries has no outlet to the sea? `227`

A	Albania
	Bangladesh **B**
C	Ecuador
	Hungary **D**

The musical *Cats* was based on a book of poems by which poet? `228`

A	Edward Lear
	Hilaire Belloc **B**
C	Lewis Caroll
	T S Eliot **D**

229 Brighton Pavilion was built by John Nash for which royal patron?

A George III

B Queen Victoria

C Prince Regent

D Edward VII

230 In which town in Normandy is there a famous tapestry depicting the Norman Conquest?

A Lisieux

B Giverney

C Bayeux

D Caen

231 The musical *My Fair Lady* was based on *Pygmalion*, a play by which playwright?

A Noel Coward

B Terence Rattigan

C G B Shaw

D Oscar Wilde

232 What sport did Marilyn Monroe's husband, Joe DiMaggio, play?

A Cricket

B American Football

C Boxing

D Baseball

Which of the following was Henry VIII's sixth and last wife? 233

A Anne Boleyn

Anne of Cleves B

C Catherine Parr

Jane Seymour D

In *The Archers* who did Hayley marry? 234

A William Grundy

Sid B

C Alistair

Roy Tucker D

Which breed of dog traditionally has its tail docked? 235

A Pembrokeshire corgi

Miniature wire-haired dachsund B

C Cardiganshire corgi

Labrador D

Which of the following was not one of the Goons? 236

A Spike Milligan

Peter Sellars B

C Harry Secombe

Bud Flanagan D

237 'Remember, remember, the Fifth of November/ Gunpowder Treason and Plot'. What was the name of the chief plotter?

A   Titus Oates

Guy Fawkes   B

C   Perkin Warbeck

The Earl of Essex   D

238 Who is the presenter of the Saturday morning radio programme *Home Truths*?

A   Melvyn Bragg

Arthur Smith   B

C   John Peel

Tony Blackburn   D

239 The winner of which golf tournament is presented with the Green Jacket?

A   The Open

Ryder Cup   B

C   US Masters

US Open   D

240 Which of these birds is unable to fly?

A   Eagle

Kiwi   B

C   Vulture

Nightingale   D

Which is the longest river in the world? 241

A Amazon

Nile B

C Mississippi

Yangtze D

John Humphries is the scourge of politicians on which daily programme? 242

A *World At One*

PM B

C *Today*

The World Tonight D

Which of the following was a famous escape artist? 243

A Papillon

Yuri Geller B

C Harry Houdini

Ronald Biggs D

Which former DJ's nickname was Fluff? 244

A Tony Blackburn

Alan Freeman B

C Jimmy Young

Jimmy Saville D

245 What variety of fruit is a Bramley?

A Apple

Banana B

C Cherry

Damson D

246 Marcel Marceau was famous as what kind of performer?

A Trapeze artist

Circus clown B

C Juggler

Mime artist D

247 The island of Majorca is ruled by which country?

A Portugal

Spain B

C Greece

Britain D

248 Louis Armstrong played which jazz instrument?

A Trombone

Tenor Sax B

C Clarinet

Trumpet D

What is the name of a type of state ruled by priests? 249

A Autocracy

Theocracy B

C Aristocracy

Gerontocracy D

'Jailhouse Rock' was one of whose famous songs? 250

A Marvin Gaye

Elvis Presley B

C Bill Haley

Jerry Lee Lewis D

Battle, a town in Sussex, derives its name from which battle? 251

A Waterloo

Hastings B

C Trafalgar

Britain D

Which production on the London stage has had the longest run? 252

A Art

An Inspector Calls B

C The Mousetrap

Cats D

253 For superstitious reasons many actors will not pronounce the title of which play?

A   *The Alchemist*

Medea   B

C   *The Iceman Cometh*

Macbeth   D

254 What was the name of the last Tsar of Russia?

A   Alexander II

Nicholas II   B

C   Peter I

Nicholas I   D

255 In a theatre what is the area with the highest seats up under the roof called?

A   Wings

Flats   B

C   Hell

Gods   D

256 In 1492, who sailed the ocean blue and discovered America?

A   Amerigo Vespucci

Henry the Navigator   B

C   Christopher Columbus

Sir Walter Raleigh   D

Which composer wrote the Brandenberg Concertos? 257

A Mozart

Liszt B

C Haydn

Bach D

In the human body, by which name is the Larynx more commonly known? 258

A Adam's Apple

Eve's Pear B

C Cain's Cherry

Abel's Artichoke D

What are the shimmering lights at the South Pole, the Southern Lights, also called? 259

A Aurora borealis

Aurora australis B

C Aurora ozus

Aurora excitealis D

Which scale is used to measure the strength of earthquakes? 260

A Beaufort scale

Brinell number B

C Richter scale

Tectonic scale D

261 Which 1956 hit for Elvis Presley has been adopted by Manchester City fans as their theme tune?

A 'Red Moon'

'Blue Moon' B

C 'Purple Moon'

'Paper Moon' D

262 'Banger' is slang for what kind of food?

A Sausage

Popcorn B

C Baked beans

Baked potatoes D

263 What is the name of Don Quixote's horse?

A Rosinante

Rosabella B

C Rosa Maria

Rosita D

264 Who said: 'Football is not a matter of life and death; it's more important than that'?

A Alex Ferguson

Alf Ramsey B

C Bob Paisley

Bill Shankly D

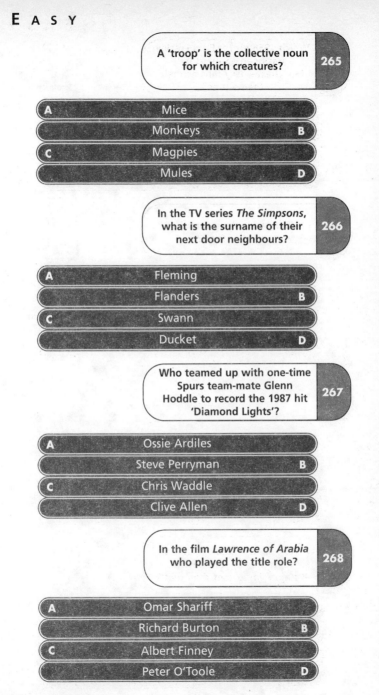

A 'troop' is the collective noun for which creatures? 265

A — Mice

Monkeys — B

C — Magpies

Mules — D

In the TV series *The Simpsons*, what is the surname of their next door neighbours? 266

A — Fleming

Flanders — B

C — Swann

Ducket — D

Who teamed up with one-time Spurs team-mate Glenn Hoddle to record the 1987 hit 'Diamond Lights'? 267

A — Ossie Ardiles

Steve Perryman — B

C — Chris Waddle

Clive Allen — D

In the film *Lawrence of Arabia* who played the title role? 268

A — Omar Shariff

Richard Burton — B

C — Albert Finney

Peter O'Toole — D

269 In which card game is it possible to make a Grand Slam?

A Poker

Canasta B

C Bridge

Racing Demon D

270 What was burnt to ashes as a memorial to English cricket after defeat by Australia in 1882?

A The losing captain

A bat B

C A ball

The bails D

271 Which animal is the symbol for the Worldwide Fund for Nature?

A Lion

Tiger B

C Giant Panda

Penguin D

272 At which Games did Cassius Clay win his Olympic heavyweight gold medal?

A 1952

1956 B

C 1960

1964 D

What is the postcode of the All England Lawn Tennis and Croquet Club? 273

A NE15

E14 B

C SW19

WC1 D

What is the cold Siberian forest known as? 274

A Moraine

Taiga B

C Drumlin

Steppe D

What type of wood are cricket bats made from? 275

A Willow

Elm B

C Oak

Mahogany D

What is supposed to act as an antidote when rubbed on a nettle sting? 276

A Parsley

Cow's lick B

C Whiskey

Dock leaf D

277 Which music did Torvill and Dean skate to when winning the Olympic gold in 1984?

A Bolero

Blue Danube B

C Skater's Waltz

Nutcracker Suite D

278 In the Old Testament, who was given a coat of many colours?

A Cain

Solomon B

C Joseph

David D

279 Whose entry increased the Five Nations Rugby Championship to six?

A Argentina

Germany B

C Italy

Spain D

280 In the play *The Rivals*, which character muddles up her long words?

A Mrs Malaprop

Mrs Palamop B

C Mrs Propamal

Mrs Pomeral D

E A S Y

Who is the patron saint of Ireland? 281

A — St Columba

St David — B

C — St Patrick

St Brendan — D

Who was the first man to run a mile in less than four minutes? 282

A — Jeffrey Archer

Roger Bannister — B

C — Jesse Owens

Sebastian Coe — D

On a musical score, what is the instruction for playing very quietly? 283

A — Allegro

Lento — B

C — Pianissimo

Andante — D

Which instrument does Larry Adler play? 284

A — Guitar

Trumpet — B

C — Piano

Harmonica — D

285 In which city is the Empire State Building?

A Chicago

Washington B

C London

New York D

286 What was the name of the gypsy girl in *The Hunchback of Notre Dame*?

A Romana

Rosita B

C Esmeralda

Petronella D

287 Which of these composers became deaf in his later years?

A Beethoven

Elgar B

C Brahms

Wagner D

288 Which actor starred in the musical film *Grease*?

A Elvis Presley

Frank Sinatra B

C Cliff Richards

John Travolta D

Yul Brynner and Deborah Kerr were the stars of which musical film?

289

A — The Sound of Music

The King and I — B

C — South Pacific

Carousel — D

In which museum is the painting of the Mona Lisa by Leonardo da Vinci housed?

290

A — National Gallery, London

National Gallery, Washington — B

C — Louvre Museum, Paris

Uffizi, Florence — D

Which British artist presented a shark in a tank of formaldehyde as a work of art?

291

A — Tracey Emin

Damien Hirst — B

C — Henry Moore

Anthony Caro — D

What is the title of Kahlil Gibran's most famous work?

292

A — The Seer

The Magus — B

C — The Sibyl

The Prophet — D

293 The ceiling of the Sistine Chapel was painted by which artist?

A Michaelangelo

Raphael B

C da Vinci

Giotto D

294 Which author created the character of George Smiley?

A Graham Greene

Evelyn Waugh B

C John le Carre

Kingsley Amis D

295 Who revisited Brideshead?

A Guy Crouchback

Charles Ryder B

C Tony Last

Anthony Blanche D

296 St Paul's Cathedral was designed by which architect?

A Sir Charles Barry

Sir Christopher Wren B

C Inigo Jones

Robert Adam D

What colour do the New Zealand rugby union team traditionally play in?

297

A   Black

Blue   B

C   Yellow

Red   D

Which ballet dancer famously defected to the West from the Soviet Union in the 1960s?

298

A   Michel Fokine

Nijinsky   B

C   Kenneth Macmillan

Rudolph Nureyev   D

In what did the Jumblies go to sea?

299

A   Pea Green Boat

Sieve   B

C   Coracle

Jam pot   D

An Oriel is what kind of architectural feature?

300

A   Door

Window   B

C   Chimney

Roof   D

301 What is the subject of the sculpture in the middle of Piccadilly Circus?

A   Lion

B   Nelson

C   Winston Churchill

D   Eros

302 The poem 'If' was written by which poet?

A   John Masefield

B   R L Stevenson

C   Rudyard Kipling

D   Walter de la Mare

303 What was the name of the dog in *The Magic Roundabout*?

A   Florence

B   Zebedee

C   Brian

D   Dougal

304 Which of the following is not a technique of painting?

A   Watercolour

B   Oil

C   Tempera

D   Stucco

What is lacking in the doldrums? **305**

A Wind

Water B

C Ice

Land D

Where in London can the National Gallery be found? **306**

A Piccadilly Circus

Parliament Square B

C Trafalgar Square

The Mall D

Which of the following is found in the brain? **307**

A Antebellum

Cerebellum B

C Terminus bellum

Belladonna D

What was the name of Babar's young cousin? **308**

A Alexander

Alfred B

C Arthur

Annabel D

309 'You can't make a silk purse out of a ...' Which of the following completes this proverb?

- A Sow's ear
- B Woolly hat
- C Paper bag
- D Potato sack

310 Graham Sutherland's tapestry 'Christ in Glory' was made for which cathedral?

- A Winchester
- B Liverpool
- C Durham
- D Coventry

311 Joanna Trollope's novels are sometimes described as what kind of sagas?

- A Lager sagas
- B Gaga sagas
- C Sexy sagas
- D Aga sagas

312 Which is the highest mountain in Western Europe?

- A Kilimanjaro
- B St Helens
- C Mont Blanc
- D K2

313 Which school do Bart and Lisa go to in the TV series *The Simpsons*?

A Springfield Elementary

B Grange Hill

C Park Hill High

D Forest Lawn Junior

314 Complete the title of this James Bond novel by Ian Fleming; *The Man with the ... Gun.*

A Smoking

B Golden

C Gatling

D Exploding

315 Who is the presenter of *Desert Island Discs*?

A Sue Lawley

B Louise Botting

C Sue Macgregor

D Jenni Murray

316 In whose memory is there a statue in the grounds of Wimbledon?

A Bunny Austin

B Fred Perry

C Arthur Ashe

D Jean Borotra

317 Emma Bunton originally acquired fame as a member of which group?

A All Saints

Atomic Kitten B

C Spice Girls

S Club Seven D

318 *An Omelette and a Glass of Wine* is a collection of the journalism of which cookery writer?

A Elizabeth David

Delia Smith B

C Jane Grigson

Rick Stein D

319 How many successive Wimbledon singles titles did Bjorn Borg win?

A Five

Two B

C Three

Eight D

320 Which Old Testament prophet was swallowed by a whale?

A Amos

Hosiah B

C Jonah

Elijah D

E A S Y

Who are the only non-English club to have won the FA Cup? `321`

A	Linfield
Glasgow Rangers	**B**
C	Cardiff City
Hibernian	**D**

In which desert do the Bushmen live? `322`

A	Atacama
Taklamakan	**B**
C	Kalahari
Kara Kum	**D**

Which famous author became Governor General of Canada as Lord Tweedsmuir? `323`

A	Walter Scott
John Buchan	**B**
C	Wilkie Collins
Anthony Trollope	**D**

What is a widgeon? `324`

A	A type of pigeon
A duck	**B**
C	A pig
A fish	**D**

325 Who killed Cock Robin?

A. Fly

B. Fish

C. Sparrow

D. Bull

326 Mrs Danvers was the housekeeper in which fictional house?

A. *Bleak House*

B. *Manderley*

C. *Barchester Towers*

D. *Northanger Abbey*

327 In what part of the world is Swahili spoken?

A. Afghanistan

B. Swaziland

C. East Africa

D. Singapore

328 According to John Masefield, what kind of a ship carried a cargo of 'Ivory,/ and apes and peacocks'?

A. Quinquereme of Nineveh

B. Stately Spanish galleon

C. Dirty British coaster

D. Clipper from Australia

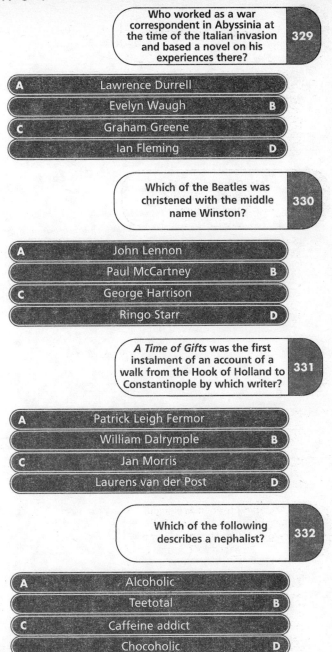

329 Who worked as a war correspondent in Abyssinia at the time of the Italian invasion and based a novel on his experiences there?

A Lawrence Durrell

B Evelyn Waugh

C Graham Greene

D Ian Fleming

330 Which of the Beatles was christened with the middle name Winston?

A John Lennon

B Paul McCartney

C George Harrison

D Ringo Starr

331 *A Time of Gifts* was the first instalment of an account of a walk from the Hook of Holland to Constantinople by which writer?

A Patrick Leigh Fermor

B William Dalrymple

C Jan Morris

D Laurens van der Post

332 Which of the following describes a nephalist?

A Alcoholic

B Teetotal

C Caffeine addict

D Chocoholic

333 Which English king was accidentally shot and killed by an arrow while hunting in the New Forest?

A William Rufus

Henry I **B**

C Richard Coeur de Lyon

John **D**

334 Nancy Mitford wrote a biography of which royal mistress?

A Madame de Maintenon

Madame de Pompadour **B**

C Mme de Montespan

Diane de Poitiers **D**

335 What is a chrysalis?

A A crystal

A developing insect **B**

C A tardis

A flower **D**

336 What is a yurt?

A An Asian tent

A South American tent **B**

C A type of cheese

A goat **D**

Which film actor is Shirley MacLaine's brother?

337

A	Burt Reynolds

	Warren Beatty	**B**

C	Ryan O'Neal

	Robert de Niro	**D**

The life of Alexander Selkirk was the inspiration behind which classic novel?

338

A	*Treasure Island*

	Robinson Crusoe	**B**

C	*Kidnapped*

	Billy Budd	**D**

What is myopia?

339

A	Short sightedness

	Long sightedness	**B**

C	A wandering eye

	A glass eye	**D**

What proverbially will happen if it rains on St Swithin's Day?

340

A	Rain for six weeks after

	No rain for six weeks after	**B**

C	Snow on Christmas Day

	Bumper harvest	**D**

341 Loftus Road is the name of which football club's home ground?

A Leicester City

B Bolton Wanderers

C Middlesborough

D Queens Park Rangers

342 What is the more usual name for a Gnu?

A Oryx

B Wildebeest

C Elk

D Caribou

343 What is a breech birth?

A A baby born headfirst

B A baby born feet first

C A baby born arms first

D A caesarean section

344 Complete the proverb 'Fine words butter no...?

A Bread

B Parsnips

C Paws

D Potatoes

Section 2:
Tricky

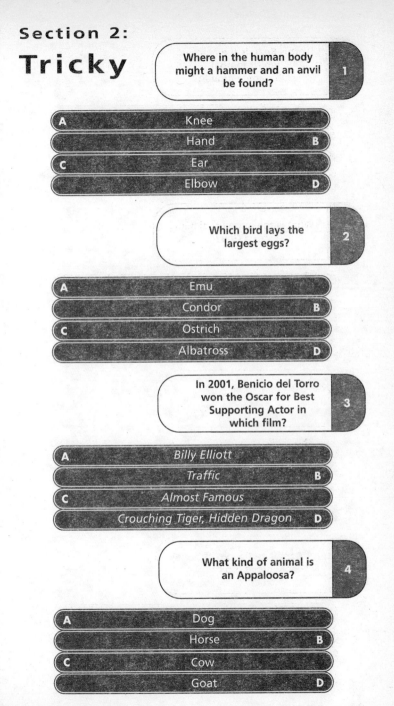

1 Where in the human body might a hammer and an anvil be found?

A Knee

B Hand

C Ear

D Elbow

2 Which bird lays the largest eggs?

A Emu

B Condor

C Ostrich

D Albatross

3 In 2001, Benicio del Torro won the Oscar for Best Supporting Actor in which film?

A *Billy Elliott*

B *Traffic*

C *Almost Famous*

D *Crouching Tiger, Hidden Dragon*

4 What kind of animal is an Appaloosa?

A Dog

B Horse

C Cow

D Goat

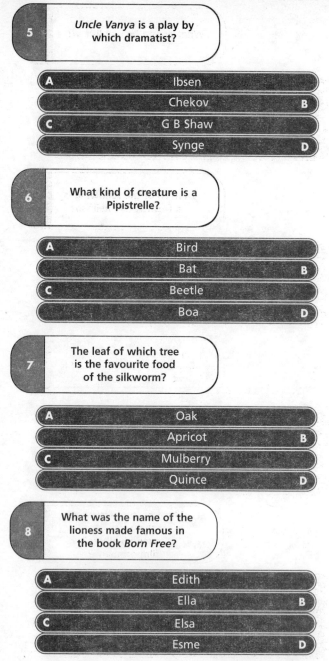

5 *Uncle Vanya* is a play by which dramatist?

A Ibsen
Chekov B
C G B Shaw
Synge D

6 What kind of creature is a Pipistrelle?

A Bird
Bat B
C Beetle
Boa D

7 The leaf of which tree is the favourite food of the silkworm?

A Oak
Apricot B
C Mulberry
Quince D

8 What was the name of the lioness made famous in the book *Born Free*?

A Edith
Ella B
C Elsa
Esme D

What does a beaver live in? 9

A	Cottage	
	Lodge	B
C	Manor	
	Bothy	D

Which of the following is a freshwater shellfish? 10

A	Lobster	
	Crab	B
C	Crayfish	
	Oyster	D

From which mythological hero did Elton John take his middle name? 11

A	Hector	
	Hercules	B
C	Achilles	
	Helen	D

Which of the following is the name of Steven Spielberg's film company? 12

A	Icon	
	Dream Works	B
C	Touchstone	
	Handmade Films	D

13 Which bird do sailors think it unlucky to kill at sea?

A Kittiwake

Stormy petrel B

C Albatross

Frigate bird D

14 In the TV sitcom *Friends* what was the name of Ross's monkey?

A Alphonse

Marcel B

C Louis

Jean-Yves D

15 What is the collective name for a group of whales?

A Herd

Flock B

C School

Muster D

16 Which actor plays the part of Erin Brokovitch's boss in the film of the same name?

A Richard Griffiths

Tom Sizemore B

C Albert Finney

Denzil Washington D

Who played the part of Private Ryan in the film *Saving Private Ryan*? `17`

A	Tom Hanks
	Ben Affleck **B**
C	Matt Damon
	Gary Sinese **D**

What is Channel Four digital channel called? `18`

A	D4
	E4 **B**
C	P4
	T4 **D**

What is the name of Milan's famous opera house? `19`

A	La Scala
	Metropolitan **B**
C	Colosseum
	Apollo **D**

Which singer released the song 'Millennium' in 2000? `20`

A	Cliff Richard
	Robbie Williams **B**
C	Madonna
	Michael Jackson **D**

21 Whose autobiography was entitled *It's All About a Ball*?

A Michael Ball
Alan Ball B
C Fred Truman
J P R Williams D

22 Nick Hornby's novel *Fever Pitch* was about supporting which football club?

A Manchester United
Arsenal B
C Tottenham
Liverpool D

23 Holkham House can be found in which English county?

A Cumbria
Somerset B
C Devonshire
Norfolk D

24 Who was the first goalkeeper to save a penalty in a Wembley FA Cup final?

A Gordon Banks
Ray Clemence B
C Bruce Grobbelaar
Dave Beasant D

TRICKY

By what name is a severe revolving storm in the China Seas known? 25

A Hurricane
Cyclone B
C Typhoon
Tornado D

Funchal is the main town on which island? 26

A Majorca
Minorca B
C Madeira
Mauritius D

In which English county is the town of Ludlow? 27

A Northumberland
Essex B
C Shropshire
Cheshire D

A waterhole in the Australian bush is known by what name? 28

A Tinny
Bayou B
C Wadi
Billabong D

29 In the harbour of which city is the statue of the Little Mermaid to be found?

A Edinburgh

Copenhagan B

C Dublin

Rotterdam D

30 Which Australian captain retired from Test cricket with a batting average of 99.94?

A Allan Border

Donald Bradman B

C Ian Chappell

Ritchie Benaud D

31 Which house belonging to the Duke of Wellington used to be known as No 1, London?

A Apsley House

Burlington House B

C Carlton House

Drayton House D

32 What geographical term describes a group of islands?

A Antipodes

Delta B

C Archipelago

Isthmus D

Tricky

How many winners did Frankie Dettori have when he went through the card at the Ascot Festival of Racing in 1996? 33

A Six

Seven B

C Eight

Nine D

The Balearic islands are to be found in which sea? 34

A Mediterranean

South China B

C Black

English Channel D

Which of these magazines is the oldest? 35

A *Punch*

Spectator B

C *Tatler*

Oldie D

Who reportedly said 'A verbal contract isn't worth the paper it's written on'? 36

A Spike Milligan

Sam Goldwyn B

C Clive Anderson

Cary Grant D

37 Of whom was Queen Victoria speaking when she said 'He speaks to me as if I were a public meeting'?

A Disraeli

Gladstone B

C Peel

Palmerston D

38 'Goodnight, sweet prince,/ And flights of angels sing thee to thy rest!' To whom are these words addressed?

A Henry V

King Lear B

C Romeo

Hamlet D

39 Complete the line 'Oh to be in England, now that ...'

A Summer's come

April's there B

C Winter's gone

Harvest's in D

40 In which city is the Spanish Riding School to be found?

A Madrid

Berlin B

C Vienna

Rome D

Which of the following completes the line 'Quoth the raven ...'?

41

A Close the door

Heed the law B

C Nevermore

Rob the poor D

In *Alice in Wonderland*, what were the flamingoes used for?

42

A Hat decorations

Lollipops B

C Croquet mallets

Stilts D

What is Silas Marner's occupation?

43

A Gamekeeper

Miller B

C Blacksmith

Weaver D

Sissinghurst is associated with which famous landscape gardener and writer?

44

A Vita Sackville-West

Rosemary Verey B

C Gertrude Jekyll

Geoffrey Jellicoe D

45 In the novel *Cry the Beloved Country*, what country is being referred to?

A Cambodia

South Africa B

C Vietnam

Russia D

46 Which planet does the moon Ganymede orbit?

A Mars

Earth B

C Jupiter

Uranus D

47 Rosalind and Orlando were the lovers in which Shakespeare play?

A *As You Like It*

The Comedy of Errors B

C *A Midsummer Night's Dream*

Twelfth Night D

48 Which of these plays were written by Chekov?

A *The Doll's House*

The Cherry Orchard B

C *The Crucible*

Journey's End D

The daughter of which American writer was married to Charlie Chaplin? 49

A   Eugene O'Neill

Neil Simon   B

C   Henry James

J D Salinger   D

In which of Dickens' novels does Mrs Sarah Gamp appear? 50

A   *Martin Chuzzlewitt*

Great Expectations   B

C   *Oliver Twist*

Nicholas Nickleby   D

In Dicken's novel *Great Expectations* in what capacity did the character Magwitch first appear? 51

A   Undertaker

Convict   B

C   Blacksmith

Beadle   D

'What immortal hand or eye/ Could frame thy fearful symmetry?' To what do Blake's lines refer? 52

A   King Cobra

Eagle   B

C   Tiger

Bear   D

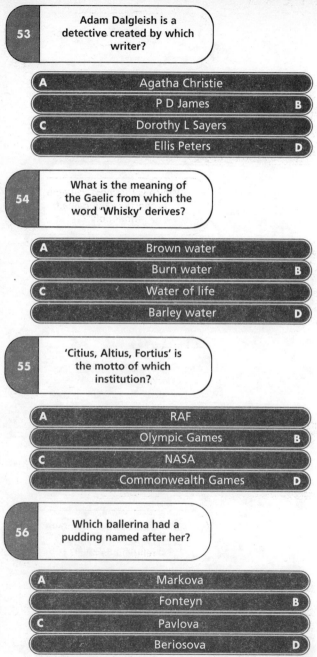

53 Adam Dalgleish is a detective created by which writer?

A Agatha Christie

P D James **B**

C Dorothy L Sayers

Ellis Peters **D**

54 What is the meaning of the Gaelic from which the word 'Whisky' derives?

A Brown water

Burn water **B**

C Water of life

Barley water **D**

55 'Citius, Altius, Fortius' is the motto of which institution?

A RAF

Olympic Games **B**

C NASA

Commonwealth Games **D**

56 Which ballerina had a pudding named after her?

A Markova

Fonteyn **B**

C Pavlova

Beriosova **D**

Amontillado is which type of wine?   57

A   Port

Sherry   B

C   Madeira

Brandy   D

Which is the most valuable property in the game, 'Monopoly'?   58

A   Regent's Street

Mile End Road   B

C   Piccadilly

Mayfair   D

Royal Flush is a term used in which pastime?   59

A   Shooting

Flirting   B

C   Poker

Golf   D

Mardi Gras is better known in England as which religious festival?   60

A   Shrove Tuesday

Ash Wednesday   B

C   Maundy Thursday

Good Friday   D

61 Who was the founder of the Scouts and Guides movement?

A Rudyard Kipling

Lord Kitchener B

C William Gladstone

Robert Baden Powell D

62 Which precious stone symbolises a fortieth wedding anniversary?

A Pearl

Ruby B

C Emerald

Sapphire D

63 What did the French royal factory at Sevres produce?

A Tapestries

Porcelain B

C Furniture

Silver D

64 What is the name of the bull in Munro Leaf's story about the bull who would not fight at the bullfights in Seville?

A Pedro

Ferdinand B

C Alfonso

Carlos D

Claret is the English name for a wine of which French region? 65

A Bordeaux
Burgundy B
C Alsace
Gascony D

Which device is used to measure and draw angles? 66

A Contractor
Extractor B
C Protractor
Distracter D

Which Napoleonic battle had a chicken dish named after it? 67

A The Nile
Austerlitz B
C Navarino
Marengo D

What is another name for an alkali? 68

A Rendezvous
Location B
C Base
Site D

69 Who showed that lightning is caused by electricity by flying a kite in a thunderstorm?

A Benjamin Franklin

Abraham Lincoln B

C President Kennedy

Charlie Chaplin D

70 What is the standard treatment for renal failure?

A A course of antibiotics

Dialysis B

C Kidney removal

Blood transfusion D

71 What was the name of the Roman goddess of love?

A Venus

Aurora B

C Vesta

Minerva D

72 What is a photovoltaic cell?

A Solar cell

Type of camera B

C Battery

Light meter D

TRICKY

73 What is the practice of freezing bodies in the hope of restoring them to life at a later date called?

A Cryonics

B Howlonics

C Weeponics

D Shoutonics

74 Which Christian sect is also known as the Latter Day Saints?

A Scientologists

B Anabaptists

C Plymouth Brethren

D Mormons

75 Who was Dolly the first cloned sheep named after?

A Dorothy Squires

B Dorothy in *The Wizard of Oz*

C Dolly Parton

D Dora Bryan

76 Whose portrait is on the back of a £20 note?

A William Shakespeare

B Sir Walter Raleigh

C Sir Edward Elgar

D Sir Christopher Wren

77 Which term is used to describe an aeroplane controlled by electronics rather than mechanics?

A Fly-by-fright

Fly-by-night B

C Fly-by-wire

Fly-by-pass D

78 Which is the holiest city and a place of pilgrimage for Muslims?

A Baghdad

Mecca B

C Teheran

Isfahan D

79 In 1588, who was in command of the Spanish Armada sent to invade England?

A Duke of Medina Sidonia

Duke of Plaza Toro B

C Don John of Austria

Duke of Parma D

80 In the Old Testament who survived the lion's den?

A Hosea

Jacob B

C Daniel

Absalom D

Which agents are thought to cause Mad Cow Disease?

81

A	Abnormal prions
	Microbes **B**
C	Flies
	Rats **D**

What was the name of a celebrated sixteenth Century French prophet?

82

A	Cassandra
	Houdini **B**
C	Nostradamus
	Clochemerle **D**

In legend, whose touch turned everything to gold?

83

A	Croesus
	Mercury **B**
C	Midas
	Medea **D**

What is the study of creatures such as the Yeti and Loch Ness Monster called?

84

A	Wildgooseology
	Cryptozoology **B**
C	Gravezoology
	Craptozoology **D**

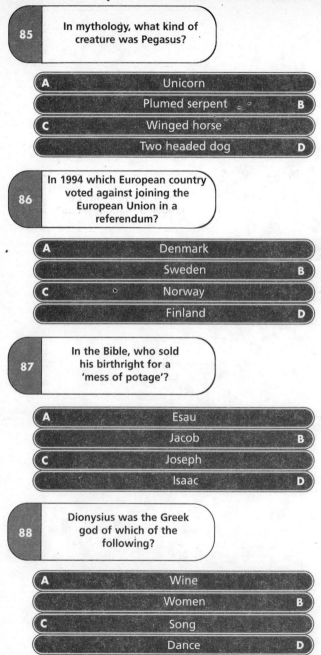

85 In mythology, what kind of creature was Pegasus?

A Unicorn

Plumed serpent B

C Winged horse

Two headed dog D

86 In 1994 which European country voted against joining the European Union in a referendum?

A Denmark

Sweden B

C Norway

Finland D

87 In the Bible, who sold his birthright for a 'mess of potage'?

A Esau

Jacob B

C Joseph

Isaac D

88 Dionysius was the Greek god of which of the following?

A Wine

Women B

C Song

Dance D

Who wrote most of the epistles in the New Testament? 89

A St Andrew

St Mark B

C St Paul

St Matthew D

In which year was the League of Nations set up? 90

A 1946

1919 B

C 1900

1871 D

Which artist was court painter to Henry VIII? 91

A Joshua Reynolds

Hans Holbein B

C Anthony Van Dyck

Peter Lely D

Who was the President of the USA from 1933–45? 92

A Calvin Coolidge

Dwight David Eisenhower B

C Franklin Delano Roosevelt

Theodore Roosevelt D

93 Which of the following was not a naval battle?

- A Trafalgar
- B The Nile
- C The Plate
- D Malplaquet

94 Which King of France was executed in the French Revolution in 1793?

- A Louis XV
- B Louis XVI
- C Charles X
- D Louis Philippe

95 In 1956 Soviet troops crushed an uprising in which country?

- A Roumania
- B Czechoslovakia
- C Hungary
- D Poland

96 Which Hebrew leader razed the city of Jericho with the blast of trumpets?

- A Aaron
- B Joshua
- C Saul
- D David

97 The siege of Ladysmith took place in which war?

A American Independence

B English Civil War

C Boer War

D World War II

98 The Great Exhibition of 1851 was housed in which building which was later burnt to the ground?

A Victoria and Albert Museum

B Crystal Palace

C Wembley Stadium

D Earls Court

99 J J Audubon was an artist renowned for his paintings of which subject?

A Roses

B Birds

C Horses

D Dogs

100 Which artist's most famous work was entitled 'The Scream'?

A Vincent van Gogh

B Hieronymus Bosch

C Edouard Munch

D Goya

101 What was the name of the last Viceroy of India?

A   Lord Curzon

Lord Lansdowne   B

C   Lord Salisbury

Lord Mountbatten   D

102 Which seventeenth Century painter was renowned for his paintings of the Spanish royal family?

A   Goya

Murillo   B

C   Titian

Velasquez   D

103 What is the name of the sculptor who created 'The Angel of the North' sited near Gateshead?

A   Rachel Whiteread

Henry Moore   B

C   Anthony Gormley

Anthony Caro   D

104 What type of creature is a grunt?

A   Pig

Fish   B

C   Monkey

Goat   D

The Pieta in St Peter's in Rome was created by which artist? 105

A	Raphael
	Bernini B
C	Michaelangelo
	Donatello D

Which of the following is not a form of English Gothic architecture? 106

A	Early English
	Decorated B
C	Norman
	Perpendicular D

Grinling Gibbons was renowned in what capacity? 107

A	Composer
	Historian B
C	Woodcarver
	Engineering D

Who was the founder of the Ballet Russe? 108

A	Michel Balanchine
	Dame Ninette de Valois B
C	Sergei Diaghilev
	Michel Fokine D

109 Which of the following is not a true insect?

A Ant

Spider B

C Beetle

Fly D

110 What is the term for a cud-chewing animal?

A Contemplative

Meditative B

C Ruminant

Philosophical D

111 What is the term for the fear of open spaces?

A Dromophobia

Claustrophobia B

C Agoraphobia

Zoophobia D

112 A dermatologist would be consulted about a problem with what part of the human body?

A Cells

Gums B

C Skin

Kidneys D

TRICKY

What kind of snake shares its name with a kind of shoe? 113

A	Sandal
B	Slipper
C	Loafer
D	Moccasin

The Lions in Trafalgar Square were sculpted by which artist? 114

A	Sir Edwin Landseer
B	Jean-Antoine Houdon
C	Antoine-Louis Barye
D	Eugene Delacroix

Which of the following is a variety of potato? 115

A	Princess Elizabeth
B	King Edward
C	Prince Hal
D	Queen Mary

An elver is the young of which creature? 116

A	Eagle
B	Elephant
C	Eel
D	Ermine

117 In a human, what type of body build does a mesomorph have?

A Tall

Fat B

C Skinny

Muscular D

118 *Helianthus* is the Latin name for which species of flower?

A Sunflower

Pinks B

C Poppy

Daffodil D

119 *Digitalis* is the Latin name for which common plant also used in medicinal drugs?

A Lady's Slipper

Buttercup B

C Foxglove

Plantain D

120 Conkers are the nuts from which tree?

A Oak

Sycamore B

C Hazel

Horse Chestnut D

121 'The ... comes in April,/ Sings his song in May/ In the middle of June/He changes his tune/And then he flies away'. Which bird?

A Swallow

Blackbird B

C Cuckoo

Martin D

122 In the film and play of *The Madness of George III*, who played the king?

A Paul Eddington

Alec Guinness B

C John Hurt

Nigel Hawthorne D

123 The Hornpipe is a dance associated with which people?

A Hunters

Bullfighters B

C Sailors

Milkmaids D

124 At which sport did Johnny 'Tarzan' Weissmuller win five Olympic gold medals?

A Long jump

High jump B

C Swimming

Synchronised swimming D

125 A Little Night Music was a musical by which composer?

A Lloyd Weber

B Noel Coward

C George Gershwin

D Stephen Sondheim

126 The song 'Some Enchanted Evening' came from which musical?

A The King and I

B South Pacific

C Evita

D My Fair Lady

127 'Sit Down, You're Rocking the Boat' was the show-stopper from which musical?

A Paint Your Wagon

B Show Boat

C Guys and Dolls

D Camelot

128 A Daddy Long Legs is also known by what name?

A Maybug

B Chafer beetle

C Crane fly

D Grasshopper

Linda Gray played which part in the TV series *Dallas*?

129

A   Miss Ellie

Pam   B

C   Sue Ellen

Jenna   D

Who played the part of Edward VIII in *Edward and Mrs Simpson*?

130

A   James Fox

Edward Fox   B

C   James Wilby

Simon Williams   D

Antonio Salieri claimed to have poisoned which rival composer?

131

A   Bach

Chopin   B

C   Mozart

Haydn   D

How many seconds had elapsed when Davide Gualtieri scored for San Marino against England in 1994 ?

132

A   Five

Seven   B

C   Nine

Twelve   D

133 Under whose rules do boxers compete?

A — Marquis de Sade

B — Marquess of Queensbury

C — Don King

D — The Queen

134 The waltz is particularly associated with which city?

A — Berlin

B — Vienna

C — Venice

D — Paris

135 Who held the world long jump record for 23 years until it was broken by Mike Powell in 1991?

A — Lynn Davies

B — Carl Lewis

C — Bob Beamon

D — Ralph Boston

136 Who was the England cricket captain at the centre of the Bodyline scandal in the 1930s?

A — Len Hutton

B — Douglas Jardine

C — Harold Larwood

D — Gubby Allen

Pompeii was destroyed by which volcano? 137

A Etna

Vesuvius B

C Santorini

Mount Pelee D

Fingal's Cave is to be found off which coast? 138

A Scotland

Ireland B

C England

Wales D

Who made the first manned space flight? 139

A Yuri Gagarin

John Glenn B

C Neil Armstrong

Buzz Aldrin D

Archangel is a port on which sea? 140

A Coral Sea

White Sea B

C Ligurian Sea

Baltic Sea D

141 What is the name of a counting device that consists of a frame holding rods and beads?

A Abacus

Accumulator B

C Diviner

Dowser D

142 Tallinn is the capital of which country?

A Albania

Estonia B

C Georgia

Turkmenistan D

143 Where would you find the Van Allen Belts?

A Sky

Boxing ring B

C Men's Outfitter

Equator D

144 Which of the following is the national symbol of Japan?

A Camellia

Pine Tree B

C Chrysanthemum

Bamboo D

'Auld Reekie' is the nickname for which Scottish city? 145

A Glasgow

Edinburgh B

C Kilmarnock

Dundee D

'Motown' is the nickname for which US city? 146

A Nashville

Chicago B

C Des Moines

Detroit D

Who pioneered the mass production of cars? 147

A John Ford

Henry Ford B

C Gerald Ford

Ford Maddox Ford D

How many sides has a heptagon? 148

A Six

Seven B

C Eight

Nine D

149 Dogger Bank is to be found in which sea?

A English Channel

North Sea B

C Irish Sea

Bristol Channel D

150 Which of these is not a celestial object?

A Quasar

Pulsar B

C Brown dwarf

Quaver D

151 Who or what is a Khamsin?

A Garment

Wind B

C Eastern ruler

Gazelle D

152 What was the name of the first test tube baby?

A John Smith

David Jones B

C Louise Brown

Gina Green D

Piraeus is the port of which city?
153

A   Tunis

Athens   B

C   Rome

Hong Kong   D

What is the name of the new orbiting space station now in construction called?
154

A   Mir

Skylab   B

C   International Space Station

Starhome   D

What type of celestial body is the Sun?
155

A   Planet

Comet   B

C   Meteorite

Star   D

What is another term for caustic soda?
156

A   Sherbet lemon

Sodium hydroxide   B

C   Depleted uranium

Key lime pie   D

157 After his abdication, the Duke of Windsor became Governor of which British colony?

- A Bermuda
- B Belize
- C The Bahamas
- D Southern Rhodesia

158 By what name was the trade union movement in Poland led by Lech Walesa known as?

- A Fidelity
- B Freedom
- C Loyalty
- D Solidarity

159 Who was the leader of the mutineers on HMS Bounty?

- A Captain Bligh
- B Billy Budd
- C Fletcher Christian
- D The Ancient Mariner

160 Which President of Egypt nationalised the Suez Canal in 1956?

- A Neguib
- B Nasser
- C Sadat
- D Mubarak

What was the name of the Russian monk, favourite of the Tsarina Alexandra, who was eventually asssinated in 1916?

161

A   Raskolnikov

Rimsky-Korsakov   **B**

C   Rasputin

Rachmaninov   **D**

Which battleground was the scene of Custer's last stand?

162

A   The Alamo

Brandywine   **B**

C   Little Big Horn

Yorktown   **D**

The Minoan civilisation was centred on which island?

163

A   Crete

Sumatra   **B**

C   Mauritius

Iona   **D**

On which island was Nelson Mandela imprisoned?

164

A   Alcatraz

Robben Island   **B**

C   Bass Rock

Devil's Island   **D**

165 Which Greek philosopher was tutor to Alexander the Great?

A Socrates

Plato B

C Aristotle

Heraclitus D

166 Which English king was killed at the Battle of Bosworth?

A Henry VI

Richard I B

C Richard III

Edward VI D

167 Napoleon Bonaparte died in exile on which island?

A Ascension

Elba B

C St Helena

Pitcairn D

168 Which Queen killed herself with the bite of an asp?

A Nefertiti

Zenobia B

C Cleopatra

Calpurnia D

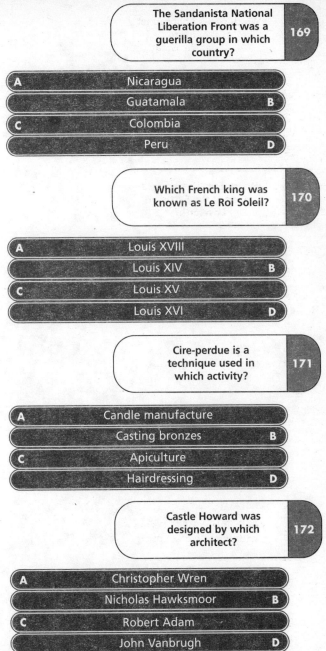

The Sandanista National Liberation Front was a guerilla group in which country? | 169

A — Nicaragua
Guatamala — B
C — Colombia
Peru — D

Which French king was known as Le Roi Soleil? | 170

A — Louis XVIII
Louis XIV — B
C — Louis XV
Louis XVI — D

Cire-perdue is a technique used in which activity? | 171

A — Candle manufacture
Casting bronzes — B
C — Apiculture
Hairdressing — D

Castle Howard was designed by which architect? | 172

A — Christopher Wren
Nicholas Hawksmoor — B
C — Robert Adam
John Vanbrugh — D

173 'Falling Water' Pennsylvania and the Guggenheim Museum, New York are two buildings designed by which architect?

A	Louis Henry Sullivan
	Walter Gropius **B**
C	Frank Lloyd Wright
	Philip Johnson **D**

174 In which city is the Hermitage Museum?

A	Paris
	St Petersburg **B**
C	Vienna
	Prague **D**

175 William Holman Hunt was part of which artistic movement?

A	Art Nouveau
	Realism **B**
C	Pre-Raphaelite Brotherhood
	Barbizon School **D**

176 Who directed the film *Reservoir Dogs*?

A	Martin Scorsese
	Stanley Kubrick **B**
C	Clint Eastwood
	Quentin Tarantino **D**

What is the word used to describe the thickness of paint on a canvas or panel? 177

A Densita

Foltezza B

C Impasto

Mistura D

Which film actor was born Archibald Leach, in Bristol? 178

A Bob Hope

James Mason B

C Cary Grant

Leslie Howard D

Which celebrated contemporary caricaturist is married to Jane Asher? 179

A Garland

Gerald Scarfe B

C Heath

David Low D

Which artist illustrated the Winnie the Pooh books? 180

A Tenniel

Arthur Rackham B

C E H Shepard

Ronald Searle D

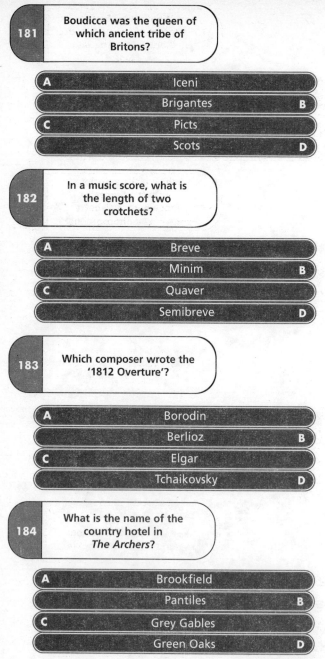

181 Boudicca was the queen of which ancient tribe of Britons?

A Iceni

Brigantes B

C Picts

Scots D

182 In a music score, what is the length of two crotchets?

A Breve

Minim B

C Quaver

Semibreve D

183 Which composer wrote the '1812 Overture'?

A Borodin

Berlioz B

C Elgar

Tchaikovsky D

184 What is the name of the country hotel in *The Archers*?

A Brookfield

Pantiles B

C Grey Gables

Green Oaks D

185 What were the first names of the two lead characters in the film *Titanic*?

A Charlie and Jane

B Eddy and Mary

C Jack and Rose

D Bill and Daisy

186 Which artist associated with the Surrealist movement was better known as a photographer?

A Max Ernst

B Man Ray

C Salvador Dali

D Tanguy

187 *The Agony and the Ecstasy* was a film about the life of which artist?

A Vincent van Gogh

B Michaelangelo

C El Greco

D Picasso

188 By what name is the technique of painting onto wet plaster known?

A Gouache

B Watercolour

C Tempera

D Fresco

189 Which is the oldest theatre still in use in London?

A Drury Lane

Haymarket B

C Garrick

Coliseum D

190 Maria Cecilia Anna Kalageropoulos was the real name of which performer?

A Margot Fonteyn

Montserrat Caballe B

C Maria Callas

Melina Mercouri D

191 In which opera were Rudolph and Mimi the tragic lovers?

A Tosca

La Boheme B

C Il Trovatore

I Pagliacci D

192 Gilbert and Sullivan's operettas were mostly performed in which London theatre?

A Apollo

Windmill B

C Savoy

Whitehall D

193 Die Fledermaus is an opera by which composer?

A	Rossini
B	Johann Strauss
C	Mozart
D	Offenbach

194 Which of these musicals was not a collaboration between Rodgers and Hammerstein?

A	Carousel
B	The King and I
C	My Fair Lady
D	South Pacific

195 The lyrics of which of these Lloyd Weber musicals were not written by Tim Rice?

A	Evita
B	Sunset Boulevard
C	Jesus Christ Superstar
D	Cats

196 How many players are there on court during a basketball game?

A	10
B	12
C	14
D	5

197 Who were partners on TV in the rag-and-bone business?

A Randall and Hopkirk

Dempsey and Makepeace B

C Cagney and Lacey

Steptoe and Son D

198 Who invariably started his programme with the catchphrase 'Hello, good evening and welcome'?

A David Frost

Bob Monkhouse B

C Hughie Green

Jess Yates D

199 In *The Archers*, what is the name of the rival pub to The Bull?

A Slug and Lettuce

Cat and Fiddle B

C Red Lion

The Felpersham Arms D

200 Who was the first Director General of the BBC?

A Lord Northcliffe

Lord Beaverbrook B

C Lord Reith

Lord Dimbleby D

201 Which stroke do swimmers perform first in the individual medley?

A	Butterfly
Breaststroke	**B**
C	Front Crawl
Backstroke	**D**

202 On which Radio channel did Chris Evans present a regular programme?

A	Virgin
Radio 1	**B**
C	Jazz FM
Capital	**D**

203 Beethoven's 'Piano Concerto No 5 in E Flat' is commonly known by what name?

A	*Moonlight*
Pathetique	**B**
C	*Pastoral*
Emperor	**D**

204 Which country do England play for cricket's Wisden Trophy?

A	Australia
Scotland	**B**
C	Sri Lanka
West Indies	**D**

205 To whom is the Venus Rosewater Dish presented each July?

A Tour de France winner

Wimbledon ladies' singles champion B

C Miss World

World snooker champion D

206 Who sang about the 'Biggest Aspidistra in the World'?

A George Formby

Benny Hill B

C Gracie Fields

June Whitfield D

207 What does a true love expect on the fifth day of Christmas?

A French hens

Gold rings B

C Turtle doves

Geese-a-laying D

208 Who performed the song 'The times they are a-changing'?

A The Beatles

Bob Dylan B

C Eric Clapton

Everley Brothers D

Who performed the song, 'Bridge over troubled water'?

209

A Don Maclean

Simon and Garfunkel B

C Abba

Eagles D

What was the name of Bill Haley's backing group?

210

A Rockers

Comets B

C Shadows

Crickets D

Isambard Kingdom Brunel designed which of these bridges?

211

A Tay

Clifton Suspension B

C Severn

Forth D

At which Grand Prix circuit are the curves Casino, Tabac and Mirabeau?

212

A Silverstone

Interlagos B

C Imola

Monaco D

213 Who held the world snooker title between 1927 and 1946?

A Ray Reardon

Walter Donaldson B

C Joe Davis

Steve Davies D

214 Henry Kelly presents a Monday to Friday radio show from 7 a.m. on which station?

A Radio 2

Capital Radio B

C Classic FM

Virgin D

215 Which discipline takes place on the last day of the Three-Day Event?

A Dressage

Cross-country B

C Showjumping

Carriage driving D

216 'Ol Man River' was a song from which musical?

A *Oklahoma*

Sweet Charity B

C *Show Boat*

Paint Your Wagon D

What is the yardage of a standard cricket pitch? 217

A 18

20 B

C 22

25 D

With which music festival was Benjamin Britten associated? 218

A Glyndebourne

Garsington B

C Aldeburgh

The Proms D

Julian Bream is noted for playing which instrument? 219

A Violin

Flute B

C Oboe

Guitar D

Which Scottish football team have their home ground in England? 220

A Stenhousemuir

Cowdenbeath B

C Berwick Rangers

Brechin City D

221 Which schoolboy is reputed to have 'invented' the game of rugby by picking up the ball and running with it?

A Arthur Conan Doyle

Tom Brown B

C Billy Bunter

William Webb Ellis D

222 Sacramento is the capital of which US state?

A California

Arizona B

C South Dakota

Florida D

223 In which sea is the island of Corfu?

A Ionian

Aegean B

C Tyrrhenian

Ligurian D

224 Which of these is not a song by the Rolling Stones?

A 'Jumping Jack Flash'

'Satisfaction' B

C 'Its all over now'

'The House of the Rising Sun' D

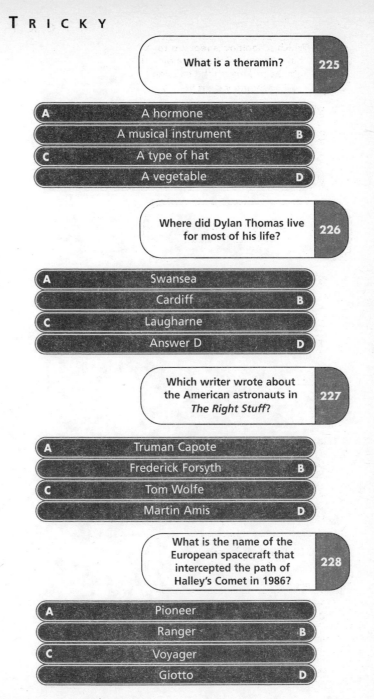

What is a theramin?
225

A · A hormone

A musical instrument · B

C · A type of hat

A vegetable · D

Where did Dylan Thomas live for most of his life?
226

A · Swansea

Cardiff · B

C · Laugharne

Answer D · D

Which writer wrote about the American astronauts in *The Right Stuff*?
227

A · Truman Capote

Frederick Forsyth · B

C · Tom Wolfe

Martin Amis · D

What is the name of the European spacecraft that intercepted the path of Halley's Comet in 1986?
228

A · Pioneer

Ranger · B

C · Voyager

Giotto · D

229 What is an atrium?

A A portal to the heart
B A dining room
C A water feature
D A kidney

230 What is the name of the heroine of The *Mill on the Floss*?

A Maggie Tulliver
B Fanny Price
C Adela Quested
D Bella Wilfer

231 Who wrote *English Passengers*?

A Matthew Kneale
B John Stoop
C David Crouchback
D Peter Prone

232 Which is the longest river in Europe?

A Danube
B Rhine
C Volga
D Rhone

Hard

What is an ocarina? 1

A	Fruit	
	Bird	**B**
C	Spanish coin	
	Wind instrument	**D**

Tito was the President of which country until his death in 1980? 2

A	Albania	
	Bulgaria	**B**
C	Yugoslavia	
	Hungary	**D**

Which breed of dog was once used for running beside coaches and carriages? 3

A	Doberman	
	Great Dane	**B**
C	Dalmation	
	Boxers	**D**

Which Irish footballer famously refused to appear as the subject of *This Is Your Life*, saying later 'I just didn't fancy it'? 4

A	George Best	
	Martin O'Neill	**B**
C	Danny Blanchflower	
	Peter Doherty	**D**

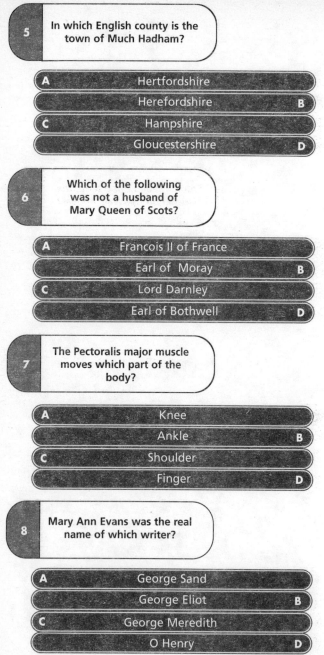

5 In which English county is the town of Much Hadham?

A   Hertfordshire

Herefordshire   **B**

C   Hampshire

Gloucestershire   **D**

6 Which of the following was not a husband of Mary Queen of Scots?

A   Francois II of France

Earl of Moray   **B**

C   Lord Darnley

Earl of Bothwell   **D**

7 The Pectoralis major muscle moves which part of the body?

A   Knee

Ankle   **B**

C   Shoulder

Finger   **D**

8 Mary Ann Evans was the real name of which writer?

A   George Sand

George Eliot   **B**

C   George Meredith

O Henry   **D**

Raskolnikov was the chief character in which novel? 9

A *Dead Souls*

Cancer Ward B

C *Crime and Punishment*

The Master and Margarita D

From where did the term, the 'Writing on the Wall' appear? 10

A Tutankhamon's tomb

Belshazzar's feast B

C The Parthenon

The Taj Mahal D

What is the cube root of 8? 11

A 2

4 B

C 32

512 D

A nymph is the young of which of these creatures? 12

A Trout

Frog B

C Dragonfly

Nightingale D

13 What was the name of the robber released in place of Jesus at the time of His trial?

A Judas

B Lazarus

C Barabbas

D Gideon

14 Who or what is a Maine Coon?

A Tree

B Cat

C Fish stew

D Motorbike

15 Which term refers to the measurement of the depth of an ocean?

A Bathymetry

B Bathypelagic

C Bathylimnetic

D Bathyscaph

16 Which TV series was originally created by the author of *Jurassic Park*, Michael Crichton?

A *ER*

B *Friends*

C *Sex in the City*

D *Dharma and Greg*

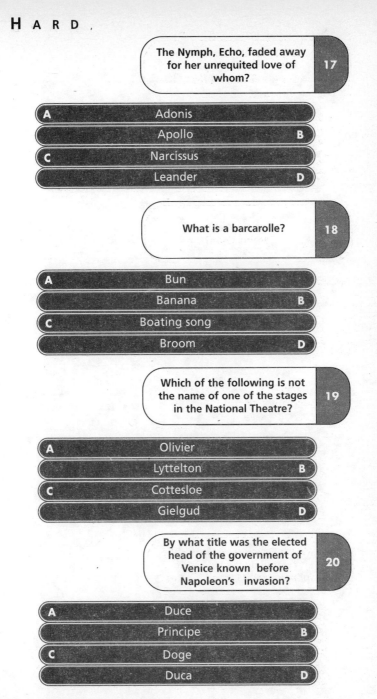

The Nymph, Echo, faded away for her unrequited love of whom? 17

- A Adonis
- B Apollo
- C Narcissus
- D Leander

What is a barcarolle? 18

- A Bun
- B Banana
- C Boating song
- D Broom

Which of the following is not the name of one of the stages in the National Theatre? 19

- A Olivier
- B Lyttelton
- C Cottesloe
- D Gielgud

By what title was the elected head of the government of Venice known before Napoleon's invasion? 20

- A Duce
- B Principe
- C Doge
- D Duca

21 *A Doll's House* was one of which playwright's most famous plays?

A	Anton Chekov
Anton Chekov	**B** G B Shaw

A Anton Chekov

B G B Shaw

C Henrik Ibsen

D Terence Rattigan

22 In which event did Sean Connery compete for Scotland in 1953?

A Rugby

B Wrestling

C Mr Universe

D Darts

23 Which artist, whose most famous painting is 'La Grande Jatte', developed a technique known as Pointillism?

A Pisarro

B Seurat

C Cezanne

D Signac

24 For her part in which film did Elizabeth Taylor win an Oscar?

A Cleopatra

B Cat on a Hot Tin Roof

C Butterfield Eight

D National Velvet

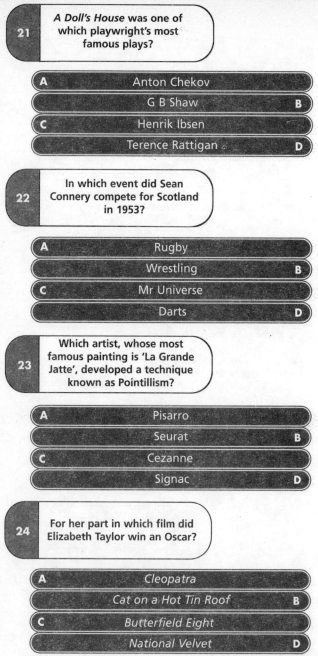

Where on a horse would you find a frog? 25

A Head

Leg B

C Hoof

Tail D

What type of creature is a Duck-billed Platypus? 26

A Reptile

Mammal B

C Bird

Fish D

Which 28-stone wrestler was christened Shirley Crabtree? 27

A Giant Haystacks

Jackie Pallo B

C Mick McManus

Big Daddy D

Which of the following has a tenor voice? 28

A Willard White

Placido Domingo B

C Chaliapin

Paul Robeson D

29 Which essential oil is often used as an insect repellant?

A   Lavender

Rosemary   B

C   Citronella

Cinnamon leaf   D

30 The opera *Eugene Onegin* was based on a novel by which Russian writer?

A   Chekov

Pushkin   B

C   Gorky

Gogol   D

31 The musical *Man of La Mancha* was based on which novel?

A   *The Three Musketeers*

Don Quixote   B

C   *Death in the Afternoon*

Our Man in Havana   D

32 Which comedy actor rowed in the Boat Race for Cambridge in 1980?

A   Mel Smith

Griff Rhys-Jones   B

C   Hugh Laurie

Rowan Atkinson   D

H A R D

Through which country does the Orinoco river flow? `33`

A	Botswana
	Malaysia **B**
C	Venezuela
	Canada **D**

Who was the founder of Island Records? `34`

A	Richard Branson
	Chris Blackwell **B**
C	Berry Gordy
	Harry Belafonte **D**

Who composed the music used by the BBC to introduce their showjumping coverage? `35`

A	Howard Goodall
	Laurie Holloway **B**
C	Mozart
	Bach **D**

What is the meaning of the phrase 'Caveat emptor'? `36`

A	Mind the hole
	No begging **B**
C	Let the buyer beware
	Not for sale **D**

37 Which Brazilian footballer was known as Little Bird?

A Pele

Zico B

C Ronaldo

Garrincha D

38 Which of these 'Lake' poets is the odd man out?

A Wordsworth

Byron B

C Coleridge

Southey D

39 Which golfer took part in the Sydney Olympic Games?

A Mark James

Severiano Ballesteros B

C Tiger Woods

Greg Norman D

40 The uncertainty principle was devised by which of the following?

A Werner Heisenberg

Albert Einstein B

C Neils Bohr

Max Planck D

Cape Cod is on the coast of which American state? 41

A Florida

California B

C South Carolina

Massachusetts D

Who used a pendulum to watch the earth rotate on its axis? 42

A Jean Foucault

Galileo B

C Copernicus

Newton D

What do the French call the English Channel? 43

A La Clanche

Notre Mer B

C La Manche

La Mer des Poissons D

Which Ohio town shares its name with a former President of the United States? 44

A McKinley

Cleveland B

C Harrison

Grant D

45 The Ponte Vecchio in Florence spans which river?

A Tiber

Arno B

C Po

Meander D

46 What kind of a creature is a Dik Dik?

A Woodpecker

Rabbit B

C Antelope

Wallaby D

47 In which city is the Topkapi Palace?

A Damascus

Baghdad B

C Islamabad

Istanbul D

48 A word which reads the same backwards as it does forwards is known by what name?

A Oxymoron

Enigma B

C Palindrome

Acrostic D

In which ocean are the Marquesas Islands where the painter Paul Gauguin once lived?

49

A   South Atlantic

Pacific   B

C   Indian

Arctic   D

In 1931 who founded the Vic-Wells Ballet company, which eventually developed into the Royal Ballet?

50

A   Frederick Ashton

Marie Rambert   B

C   Ninette de Valois

Anthony Tudor   D

In which story does Mrs Doasyouwouldbedoneby make an appearance?

51

A   *Rewards and Fairies*

Peter Pan   B

C   *The Water Babies*

The Wind in the Willows   D

Against which country did Australia score 31 goals, without reply, in a World Cup qualifying match in 2001?

52

A   England

American Samoa   B

C   Western Samoa

Papua New Guinea   D

53 Which scale is used for estimating wind speeds?

A Marlborough

Buccleuch B

C Beaufort

Monmouth D

54 'Rose red city, half as old as time'. This line refers to which city?

A Palmyra

Babylon B

C Petra

Baghdad D

55 In 1876 Richard Wagner founded an annual music festival devoted to the performance of his own works in which town?

A Munich

Salzburg B

C Bayreuth

Drottningholm D

56 On which river is the city of Lisbon situated?

A Tagus

Douro B

C Arno

Neva D

57 'The quality of mercy is not strained/ It droppeth as the gentle rain.' From which of Shakespeare's plays do these lines come?

- **A** Twelfth Night
- **B** Macbeth
- **C** The Merchant of Venice
- **D** Othello

58 What is an inhabitant of Monaco known as?

- **A** Monaque
- **B** Monacoan
- **C** Monegasque
- **D** Monache

59 What was the name of the brothers who made the first manned flight?

- **A** Wright
- **B** Montgolfier
- **C** Zeppelin
- **D** Cayley

60 *Superior Person* was the title of Kenneth Rose's biography of which Lord?

- **A** Lord Palmerston
- **B** Lord Salisbury
- **C** Lord Melbourne
- **D** Lord Curzon

61 What was the name of the Suffolk village that Ronald Blythe wrote a portrait of?

A Akenfield

B Brympton

C Chadiston

D Duckleburgh

62 The metacarpals are bones found in which part of the human body?

A Ear

B Knee

C Legs

D Hands

63 Which fictional detective was created by Simenon?

A Inspector Clouseau

B Maigret

C Hercule Poirot

D Alphonse Prideaux

64 Complete the saying, 'Neither fish, nor fowl, nor good ...'?

A Red rabbit

B Green beans

C Red herring

D Bluebottle

Where is the Mojave Desert? `65`

A New Mexico	
Mexico	**B**
C California	
Arizona	**D**

'The Lord is a shoving leopard': Which Warden of an Oxford college had a tendency to transpose letters in this way? `66`

A Maurice Bowra	
John Sparrow	**B**
C Lewis Carroll	
The Reverend William Spooner	**D**

What is the prediction for Thursday's child? `67`

A Fair of face	
Loving and giving	**B**
C Far to go	
Full of grace	**D**

Who was the composer of the opera *Otello*? `68`

A Mozart	
Rossini	**B**
C Puccini	
Verdi	**D**

69 What is known as the Fourth Estate?

A   Balmoral

Northern Ireland   B

C   The Hoi Polloi

The Press   D

70 Cassis is spirit flavoured with which fruit?

A   Raspberry

Blackcurrant   B

C   Apple

Plum   D

71 Who wrote 'The female of the species is more deadly than the male'?

A   Rudyard Kipling

Charles Darwin   B

C   Germaine Greer

Oscar Wilde   D

72 A Hamadryad is another name for which snake?

A   Black Mamba

King Cobra   B

C   Anaconda

Coral snake   D

Which of these men did Scarlet O'Hara not marry? 73

A   Charles Hamilton

Ashley Wilkes   B

C   Rhett Butler

Frank Kennedy   D

Which is the longest navigable canal in the world? 74

A   Grand Canal, China

Suez   B

C   Kiel

Panama   D

There were three men in a boat and a dog. What was the name of the dog? 75

A   George

Montmorency   B

C   Harris

J   D

Who was the presenter of the documentary art series, *Civilisation*? 76

A   Robert Hughes

Huw Weldon   B

C   Kenneth Clark

Bamber Gascoigne   D

77 Who wrote the play
Who's Afraid of Virginia Woolf?

A Arthur Miller	
Tom Stoppard	**B**
C Michael Frayn	
Edward Albee	**D**

78 What does the term 'en croute' mean?

A In pastry	
Framed	**B**
C Pregnant	
Buried	**D**

79 What was Shakespeare's last play?

A *The Comedy of Errors*	
The Winter's Tale	**B**
C *The Tempest*	
Love's Labours Lost	**D**

80 A hinny is the young of which animal?

A Beaver	
Ass	**B**
C Whale	
Rhinoceros	**D**

Fair Isle knitwear originates from which group of islands?

81

A Orkneys

Shetlands B

C Arran

Hebrides D

In which play does the character Mrs Ogmore Pritchard appear?

82

A *Under Milk Wood*

Blithe Spirit B

C *Separate Tables*

The Importance of Being Earnest D

Who was the author of the novel *The Age of Innocence*?

83

A J M Barrie

Edith Wharton B

C E M Forster

Rosamund Lehmann D

Which of the following is not a form of pasta?

84

A Linguine

Risotto B

C Macaroni

Farfalle D

85 What would you do with a Baklava?

A Wear it	
Eat it	**B**
C Fire it	
Sit on it	**D**

86 Which of these is not one of the three sisters in Chekov's play of the same name?

A Olga	
Natasha	**B**
C Masha	
Irina	**D**

87 What is the name of the bottle which can hold eight bottles of wine?

A Balthazar	
Jeroboaom	**B**
C Methuselah	
Magnum	**D**

88 Who said 'Reports of my death have been greatly exaggerated'?

A Saddam Hussein	
Duke of Wellington	**B**
C Dr Livingstone	
Mark Twain	**D**

Ermine is the winter coat of which animal? 89

A Seal

Fox B

C Stoat

Sable D

What was the name of 'the doll' in Ibsen's play *The Doll's House*? 90

A Mina

Ellen B

C Annie

Nora D

Which race course is also the name of a card game? 91

A Kempton

Towcester B

C Newmarket

Doncaster D

Moss stitch is used in which form of needlework? 92

A Embroidery

Petit point B

C Knitting

Crochet D

93 Which branch of logic describes imprecise reasoning and knowledge so it can be handled by a computer?

A Hairy logic

Furry logic B

C Bald logic

Fuzzy logic D

94 Which Greek island was the home of Odysseus?

A Corfu

Cyprus B

C Ithaca

Cephalonia D

95 Which radio astronomer discovered the first pulsar?

A Gertrude Bell

Acton Bell B

C Alexander Graham Bell

Jocelyn Bell D

96 What word is used to describe a sexually excited elephant?

A Musth

Mushy B

C Moony

Mouldy D

H A R D

What is Luciferin? 97

A	Match
B	Devil's disciple
C	Glowing substance in glow-worms
D	Rebellious angel

What kind of creature is a Cockchafer? 98

A	Bird
B	Beetle
C	Boa constrictor
D	Bison

In computing, what is the term for a single digit of binary notation represented by either a 0 or a 1? 99

A	Nibble
B	Byte
C	Bit
D	Bitmap

Which chemicals are the building blocks of proteins? 100

A	Nucleic acids
B	Amino acids
C	Enzymes
D	Hormones

101 Which chromosome distinguishes men from women?

A X

Y B

C W

Z D

102 Which of these is not a pachyderm?

A Elephant

Gorilla B

C Hippopotamus

Rhinoceros D

103 What is MRSA?

A Medical degree

Resistant bacterium B

C Aeroplane

Missile D

104 What is a Gila monster?

A Lizard

Dinosaur B

C Fish

Mythical creature D

H A R D

What is a Samoyed? 105

A   Canoe

Eskimo   B

C   Dog

Garment   D

What temperature is absolute zero? 106

A   –459.67 C

0 C   B

C   –1000C

–273.15C   D

What is a cichlid? 107

A   Plant

Insect   B

C   Fungus

Fish   D

Divali or the Festival of Lights celebrates what event for Hindus? 108

A   New Year

Spring   B

C   Birth of Rama

Birth of Krishna   D

109 A Unicorn will only allow itself to be caught by what?

A Golden halter

Virgin maid B

C Handful of manna

Cupful of nectar D

110 Which of the authors of the four gospels of the New Testament was not Jewish?

A Matthew

Mark B

C Luke

John D

111 What is another name for Mother Carey's Chickens?

A Bantams

Stormy petrels B

C Flying fish

Fireflies D

112 'Work expands so as to fill the time available for its completion.' Whose law is this?

A Aspel

Parkinson B

C Wogan

Paxman D

113 Lafayette Ron Hubbard founded which religious movement?

A   Unification Church

Theosophy   B

C   Scientology

Christian Science   D

114 What was Oedipus' blood relationship with his wife, Jocasta?

A   Father

Son   B

C   Brother

Uncle   D

115 Which British dramatist wrote *The Caretaker*?

A   John Osborne

Arnold Wesker   B

C   Harold Pinter

Terence Rattigan   D

116 In the Judgement of Paris, who was 'the fairest'?

A   Athena

Hera   B

C   Aphrodite

Helen   D

117 What effect does the substance Gibberellin have?

A	Makes us laugh
	Makes plants grow **B**
C	Makes birds sing
	Makes monkey chatter **D**

118 Who ruled as dictator of Spain from the Civil War until his death in 1975?

A	Franco
	Trujillo **B**
C	Mussolini
	Batista **D**

119 Who was the first director of the National Theatre?

A	Peter Hall
	Lawrence Olivier **B**
C	Trevor Nunn
	Henry Irving **D**

120 Who was known as the Winter Queen?

A	Christina of Sweden
	Elizabeth of Bohemia **B**
C	Margaret of Anjou
	Marie Antoinette of France **D**

Haile Selassie was emperor of which country from 1930-1974?

121

A	Afghanistan
	Madagascar B
C	Ethiopia
	Persia D

Jim Hacker ended up in which high office of state?

122

A	Foreign Secretary
	Home Secretary B
C	Prime Minister
	Chancellor of the Exchequer D

Which British poet died of malaria during the Greek War of Independance?

123

A	Rupert Brooke
	Lord Byron B
C	Percy Bysshe Shelley
	Samuel Taylor Coleridge D

By what name are baby rabbits known?

124

A	Pups
	Kittens B
C	Cubs
	Fawns D

125 Which port is the capital of Papua New Guinea?

A Port Elizabeth

Port Moresby B

C Port Harcourt

Port Arthur D

126 Whose image appeared on the famous World War I recruitment poster 'Your Country Needs You'?

A General Charles Gordon

Lloyd George B

C Kitchener

Winston Churchill D

127 Who was responsible for the massacre of the Israeli athletes at the Munich Olympics in 1972?

A Black Panthers

Black September B

C Black Hand

Black Death D

128 In the Kipling's *Jungle Book*, what kind of a snake was Kaa?

A Cobra

Python B

C Rattlesnake

Grass snake D

H ARD

What was the name of the leader of the Peasants Revolt triggered by the imposition of a Poll Tax in 1380? 129

A	Wat Tyler
B	Jack Dauber
C	Sam Baler
D	Tom Farmer

Clematis Vitalba is the Latin name of which common hedgerow plant? 130

A	Ragged Robin
B	Love in a mist
C	Leopardsbane
D	Old Man's Beard

In World War II 'Quisling' was a term for a traitor deriving from the name of the Fascist leader from which country? 131

A	Turkey
B	Norway
C	Finland
D	Japan

What is a Cassowary? 132

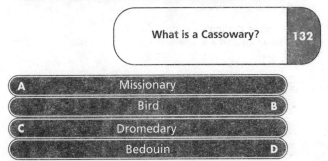

A	Missionary
B	Bird
C	Dromedary
D	Bedouin

133 Which portrait painter epitomised the glamour of the Edwardian age in English high society?

A   Dante Gabriel Rossetti

James McNeill Whistler   B

C   Augustus John

John Singer Sargent   D

134 In the film *Sunset Boulevard* Norma Desmond was played by which actress?

A   Joan Crawford

Marlene Dietrich   B

C   Gloria Swanson

Bette Davies   D

135 The work of the architect Gaudi is mostly to be found in which city?

A   Turin

Barcelona   B

C   Avignon

Vienna   D

136 Which singer famous in the 1960s converted to Islam?

A   Mike D'Abo

Dave Clark   B

C   Donovan

Cat Stevens   D

Which adjective describes a 'crinkle-crankle' wall? 137

A Castellated

Uneven B

C Serpentine

Defensive D

Who was the first president of the Royal Academy? 138

A Lord Burlington

Prince Albert B

C Sir Joshua Reynolds

Sir Anthony van Dyck D

'Over the Rainbow', one of Judy Garland's most famous songs, came from which film? 139

A The Wizard of Oz

A Star is Born B

C Meet Me in St Louis

Easter Parade D

What is the bracket on the underside of a hinged choir stall called which supports the occupant while standing? 140

A Clerestory

Misericord B

C Reredos

Transept D

141 Which body of water lies between the Mediterranean and the Black Sea?

A   Ionian Sea

Sea of Marmara   B

C   Caspian Sea

Aegean Sea   D

142 Who played the part of Blanche Du Bois in the film *A Streetcar Named Desire*?

A   Elizabeth Taylor

Vivien Leigh   B

C   Joan Crawford

Katharine Hepburn   D

143 The 'Rokeby Venus' was painted by which artist?

A   Titian

Ingres   B

C   Velasquez

Manet   D

144 Which cells in the body contain the enzyme acetylcholinesterase?

A   Muscle

Bone   B

C   Nerve

Skin   D

In 1917 Marcel Duchamp exhibited a urinal to which he gave what title? 145

A Waterfall

Rain B

C Fountain

Outflow D

What is used to make vellum? 146

A Linen

Animal skin B

C Papyrus

Wood pulp D

In which of these TV series did the character of Chrystal Carrington appear? 147

A *Dallas*

Dynasty B

C *Baywatch*

Neighbours D

Which of the following cannot be prefixed with the word 'tiger' to make a living creature? 148

A Beetle

Moth B

C Monkey

Shark D

149 Which king of England carried off the Stone of Scone from Scotland to England?

A	William the Conqueror
B	Henry II
C	Edward I
D	Richard III

150 In Kipling's *Jungle Book*, what kind of creature was Riki Tiki Tavi?

A	Monkey
B	Deer
C	Mongoose
D	Bird

151 Which of these sub-species of Tiger is now extinct?

A	Bengal
B	Siberian
C	Sumatran
D	Caspian

152 What is an Avocet?

A	Lawyer
B	Fruit
C	Bird
D	Aeroplane

Who was Romeo in the Florida film version of Shakespeare's play? **153**

A | Mat Damon
Leonardo di Caprio | **B**
C | Johnny Depp
Vinnie Jones | **D**

What sort of creature is the Devil's Coach-horse? **154**

A | Crab
Beetle | **B**
C | Bird
Shetland pony | **D**

Which British politician established the Metropolitan Police in the mid-nineteenth Century? **155**

A | Lord Melbourne
Duke of Wellington | **B**
C | Sir Robert Peel
Benjamin Disraeli | **D**

What was the name of the white horse who helped to clear the Wembley pitch of spectators at the 1923 Cup final? **156**

A | Billie
Snowy | **B**
C | Chalky
Desert Orchid | **D**

157 Which of the following is an evil smelling fungus?

A Stinkard

Stinkhorn B

C Stinkwood

Stinkweed D

158 Which caricaturist is best known for his series of drawings of embarrassing 'The Man Who ...' situations.

A Giles

Gilray B

C H M Bateman

Pont D

159 In which film did troops go into battle to the sound of 'The Ride of the Valkyrie'?

A *The Deerhunter*

Saving Private Ryan B

C *Apocalypse Now*

The Longest Day D

160 Which is the shortest time period of the following?

A Millisecond

Microsecond B

C Femtosecond

Attosecond D

**Who directed the film
The Third Man?** 161

A	Orson Welles
Alfred Hitchcock	B
C	Carol Reed
David Lean	D

**Which of the Great Lakes is in
the United States of America?** 162

A	Superior
Huron	B
C	Michigan
Erie	D

**Which composer wrote the
music for the ballet,
The Rite of Spring?** 163

A	Prokofiev
Satie	B
C	Poulenc
Stravinsky	D

**What is the name of the
European spacecraft that
intercepted the path of
Halley's Comet in 1986?** 164

A	Pioneer
Ranger	B
C	Voyager
Giotto	D

165 Which opera was written for the opening of the Suez Canal and had its premiere in Egypt?

A *Die Aegyptische Helena*

Aida B

C *Die Zauberflote*

Die Entfuhrung aus dem Serail D

166 Who caused a heavyweight boxing sensation in 1990 when he knocked out Mike Tyson in Tokyo?

A Buster Bloodvessel

James 'Buster' Douglas B

C Douglas Bader

Buster Edwards D

167 Which of these diseases affects men only?

A Haemophilia

Hydrophobia B

C Hypertension

Haemorrhoids D

168 Which annual arts festival was founded in 1947 by Rudolph Bing?

A Salzburg

Venice Biennale B

C Edinburgh

Garsington D

On which river is the city of Baghdad situated? 169

A	Tiber
Tigris	B
C	Indus
Tagus	D

'No man is an island'. Whose words are these? 170

A	Winston Churchill
John Donne	B
C	John Milton
Alexander Pope	D

Baron Scarpia is the Chief of Police in which opera? 171

A	Tosca
I Vespri Siciliani	B
C	Simon Boccanegra
Il Trovatore	D

Who was riding Devon Loch when the horse collapsed just before the winning post in the 1956 Grand National? 172

A	John Oaksey
Dick Francis	B
C	Fred Archer
Scobie Breasley	D

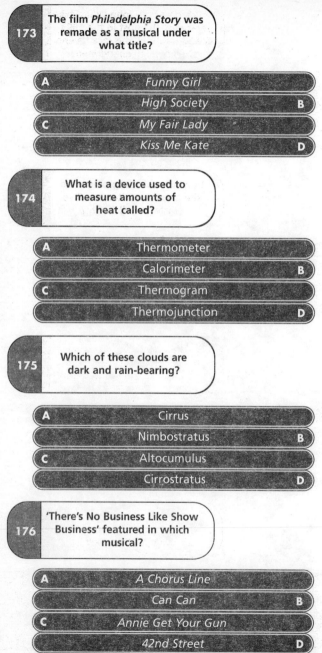

173 The film *Philadelphia Story* was remade as a musical under what title?

A · *Funny Girl*

High Society · B

C · *My Fair Lady*

Kiss Me Kate · D

174 What is a device used to measure amounts of heat called?

A · Thermometer

Calorimeter · B

C · Thermogram

Thermojunction · D

175 Which of these clouds are dark and rain-bearing?

A · Cirrus

Nimbostratus · B

C · Altocumulus

Cirrostratus · D

176 'There's No Business Like Show Business' featured in which musical?

A · *A Chorus Line*

Can Can · B

C · *Annie Get Your Gun*

42nd Street · D

177 Which horse did John White take first-past-the-post in the 1993 Grand National, the race having already been abandoned?

A Mr Frisk

Rough Quest B

C Esha Ness

Lord Gyllene D

178 In which quiz programme did the presenter often say 'I've started so I'll finish'?

A Brain of Britain

Twenty Questions B

C University Challenge

Mastermind D

179 Kaolin and petuntse are the basic ingredients needed to produce what kind of material?

A Glass

Stoneware B

C Hard paste porcelain

Terracotta D

180 Which of Napoleon's marshals became King of Sweden?

A Ney

Bernadotte B

C Massena

Murat D

181 Who ran stark naked round Piccadilly Circus on Red Nose Day 2001?

A   Jordan

Billy Connolly   B

C   Jo Brand

Martin Clunes   D

182 What was the name of the family in the *Darling Buds of May*?

A   Amis

Eliot   B

C   Larkin

Pound   D

183 The poem 'Adonais' was written by Shelley in memory of which other poet?

A   Byron

Spenser   B

C   Keats

Milton   D

184 Who is the presenter of the radio programme *Loose Ends*?

A   John Peel

Michael Buerk   B

C   Ned Sherrin

Libby Purves   D

Whose voice do listeners wake up to every weekday morning on Radio 2? 185

A Chris Tarrant

Jonathan Ross B

C Jimmy Young

Terry Wogan D

The music for *Land of Hope and Glory* was written by which composer? 186

A Thomas Arne

Arthur Sullivan B

C Edward Elgar

Gustav Holst D

Sir Thomas Beecham founded which orchestra? 187

A Halle

London Philharmonic B

C Chicago Symphony

New York Philharmonic D

Leon Goossens was noted for playing which instrument? 188

A Harpsichord

Violin B

C Oboe

Piano D

189 Which of these Wagner operas do not form part of *The Ring*?

A	*Das Rheingold*
B	*Die Meistersingers*
C	*Siegfried*
D	*Die Walkyrie*

190 Lieutenant Pinkerton betrays the heroine of which opera?

A	*Madame Butterfly*
B	*The Girl of the Golden West*
C	*Arabella*
D	*The Bartered Bride*

191 What would you do with a cembalo?

A	Eat it
B	Plant it
C	Play it
D	Wear it

192 The Taj Mahal at Agra was built by which emperor?

A	Jahangir
B	Haile Selassie
C	Genghis Khan
D	Shah Jehan

193 Which sprinter, immortalised in the film *Chariots of Fire*, went on to become an athletics administrator?

A Linford Christie

Harold Abrahams B

C Eric Liddell

Allan Wells D

194 Which singer became Mayor of Palm Springs?

A Frank Sinatra

Sonny Bono B

C Sammy Davis

Frankie Lane D

195 In which particular aspect of painting did Nicholas Hilliard specialise?

A Landscapes

Murals B

C Portrait Miniatures

Seascapes D

196 Which British singer became known as the 'Forces' Sweetheart' in World War II?

A Gracie Fields

Rosemary Clooney B

C Vera Lynn

Jessie Matthews D

197 Who directed the film *Crouching Tiger, Hidden Dragon*?

A Chow Yun Fat

Michelle Yeoh B

C Ang Lee

Zhang Ziyi D

198 Which monarch founded the Royal Hospital, Chelsea as an asylum for old soldiers?

A Henry VII

Charles II B

C Queen Anne

George III D

199 Mozambique is a former colony of which country?

A France

Spain B

C Portugal

Britain D

200 Where did the greatest ever recorded eruption of a volcano take place in 1883?

A Mount Pelee

Mount St Helens B

C Popacatapetl

Krakatoa D

In the novel *The Scarlet Letter* which is the letter? 201

- **A** A for Adultery
- **B** B for Bestiality
- **C** C For Cuckold
- **D** D for Devil Worshipper

Which semi-precious stone has the same name as a range of mountains? 202

- **A** Garnet
- **B** Zagros
- **C** Cairngorm
- **D** Agate

What type of creature is a Basenji? 203

- **A** Cat
- **B** Chicken
- **C** Goat
- **D** Dog

Fanny Brice was the inspiration for which musical? 204

- **A** *The Girl Friend*
- **B** *The BoyFriend*
- **C** *Funny Girl*
- **D** *Hello Dolly*

205 Romansch is a language spoken in which European country?

A Spain

Switzerland B

C Austria

France D

206 'Mister Softee' was the show jumper belonging to which rider?

A Mary Gordon Watson

Pat Smythe B

C David Broome

Caroline Bradley D

207 The painting known as 'The Arnolfini Marriage' was painted by which artist?

A Jan van Eyck

Rogier van der Weyden B

C Pieter Brueghel

Cranach D

208 Who invented the characters Mapp and Lucia?

A Ronald Firbank

P G Wodehouse B

C E F Benson

Mrs Gaskell D

Which French novelist wrote *Madame Bovary*? 209

A	Prosper Merimee
	Gustave Flaubert **B**
C	The Goncourt brothers
	Colette **D**

Which Football League club did Ian Botham play for? 210

A	Leeds
	Scunthorpe **B**
C	Bristol City
	Bournemouth **D**

In Tennyson's poem, who lived on an island in a river near Camelot? 211

A	Maud
	Lady Clara Vere de Vere **B**
C	The Lady of Shalott
	The Lotus Eaters **D**

Which river flows through the Grand Canyon? 212

A	Colorado
	Rio Grande **B**
C	Delaware
	Missouri **D**

213 Which sport takes place at Bisley?

A	Archery	
	Darts	B
C	Croquet	
	Shooting	D

214 Which of these plays is not by G B Shaw?

A	*Pygmalion*	
	Arms and the Man	B
C	*Mother Courage*	
	Major Barbara	D

215 Which island is the largest producer of cloves?

A	Guam	
	Curacao	B
C	Zanzibar	
	Sulawesi	D

216 Who 'Told such dreadful lies, it made one gasp and stretch ones eyes'?

A	Augusta	
	Amelia	B
C	Matilda	
	Susanna	D

HARD

217 What is John le Carre's real name?

- A   Edward Kent
- B   David Cornwall
- C   Andrew Devonshire
- D   Bernard Norfolk

218 Katsushika Hokusai is celebrated in which field?

- A   Politics
- B   Painting
- C   Architecture
- D   Literature

219 Which scientist wrote the *Principia Mathematica*?

- A   Galileo
- B   Leibnitz
- C   Hooke
- D   Newton

220 The play *The Second Mrs Tanqueray* was written by which playwright?

- A   Sir Arthur Pinero
- B   Oscar Wilde
- C   G B Shaw
- D   Terence Rattigan

221 Which inventor built a calculating machine that anticipated the modern computer?

A Heath Robinson

Charles Babbage **B**

C Thomas Edison

Leonardo da Vinci **D**

222 In the film *Kind Hearts and Coronets* which actor played all eight members of the D'Ascoyne family?

A Peter Sellars

Lawrence Olivier **B**

C Alec Guinness

Ralph Richardson **D**

223 Which would-be invader referred to the English Channel as a 'mere ditch'?

A Hitler

Julius Caesar **B**

C William of Normandy

Napoleon **D**

224 'Let the Sunshine In' was a song from which musical?

A *Oklahoma*

Salad Days **B**

C *The Sound of Music*

Hair **D**

Section 4:
Very
Difficult

In the TV series, *Clarissa and the Countryman*, who was the Countryman? 1

A   Johnny Scott

   Toby Welsh   B

C   Geordie Kent

   David Cornwall   D

Which hereditary disease caused the 'madness' of George III? 2

A   Haemophilia

   Porphyria   B

C   Cystic fibrosis

   Huntingdon's Chorea   D

Virginia Woolf's *Orlando* was based on which real person? 3

A   Violet Trefusis

   Radclyffe Hall   B

C   Vita Sackville-West

   Lord Alfred Douglas   D

The Oaks is one of the two classic races for fillies only. Which is the other? 4

A   1000 Guineas

   The Derby   B

C   2000 Guineas

   St Leger   D

5 Philately is another name for the hobby of collecting what?

A Cigarette cards

Bird's eggs B

C Stamps

Butterflies D

6 Which English cathedral has a clock with no face?

A Lincoln

Durham B

C Salisbury

Winchester D

7 Lapis lazuli used to be ground up to make which pigment?

A Cerulean blue

Prussian blue B

C Indigo

Ultramarine D

8 The Hanging Gardens of Babylon were built by which King?

A Alexander the Great

Genghis Khan B

C Nebuchadnezzar

Cyrus the Great D

VERY DIFFICULT

What was the name of the yacht on which Sir Francis Chichester sailed solo around the world in 1966–7?

9

A	Cutty Sark
	Kingfisher **B**
C	Mayflower
	Gipsy Moth IV **D**

What is the Oriental art of growing dwarf plants known as?

10

A	Ikebana
	Origami **B**
C	Bonsai
	Kendo **D**

What 'In some melodious plot/ Of beechen green, and shadows numberless/ Singest of summer in full-throated ease'?

11

A	The Lark
	The Nightingale **B**
C	The Cuckoo
	The Blackbird **D**

'We that are young/ Shall never see so much nor live so long.' These are the last lines of which Shakespeare play?

12

A	The Tempest
	Macbeth **B**
C	King Lear
	A Winter's Tale **D**

13 What do phycologists study?

- A Blood
- B Algae
- C Pigments
- D Leaves

14 Which is the only bird that can fly backwards?

- A Toucan
- B Kestrel
- C Hummingbird
- D Canary

15 Lake Ladoga can be found in which country?

- A Italy
- B Chile
- C Alaska
- D Russia

16 Who wrote the play *Amadeus* about the rivalry between Salieri and Mozart?

- A Peter Shaffer
- B Harold Pinter
- C Tom Stoppard
- D Anthony Shaffer

17 Richard Ingrams, who used to edit *Private Eye*, is now the editor of which magazine?

A Spectator

B New Statesman

C The Oldie

D Punch

18 'Cogito, ergo sum'. Which philosopher is associated with that formulation?

A Spinoza

B Descartes

C Nietzsche

D Plato

19 Positron Emission Tomography is used to study which of the following?

A Nuclear reactions

B Pollution

C Climate change

D Brain function

20 In 1853, the United States of America bought which state from Mexico by means of the Gadsden Purchase?

A Montana

B Arizona

C South Dakota

D California

21 *Boule de Suif* was written by which French novelist?

A   Guy de Maupassant

Emile Zola   **B**

C   Victor Hugo

Honore de Balzac   **D**

22 The illustrator Aubrey Beardsley was associated with which artistic movement?

A   Arts and Crafts

Art Deco   **B**

C   Art Nouveau

Art Now   **D**

23 Who starred with Gary Cooper in the western, *High Noon*?

A   Barbara Stanwyck

Carole Lombard   **B**

C   Grace Kelly

Katharine Hepburn   **D**

24 Which is the odd man out among these 'Beat Generation' writers?

A   Robert Lowell

William Burroughs   **B**

C   Alan Ginsberg

Jack Kerouac   **D**

Which Egyptian god had the head of a jackal?

25

A   Horus

Thoth   B

C   Anubis

Ammon   D

On which racecourse is there a statue of the legendary steeplechaser Arkle?

26

A   Aintree

Cheltenham   B

C   Newbury

Chepstow   D

In which country are the Drakensberg Mountains?

27

A   Rumania

South Africa   B

C   Canada

Switzerland   D

Which Russian author wrote the story of The Queen of Spades?

28

A   Gogol

Tolstoy   B

C   Turgenev

Pushkin   D

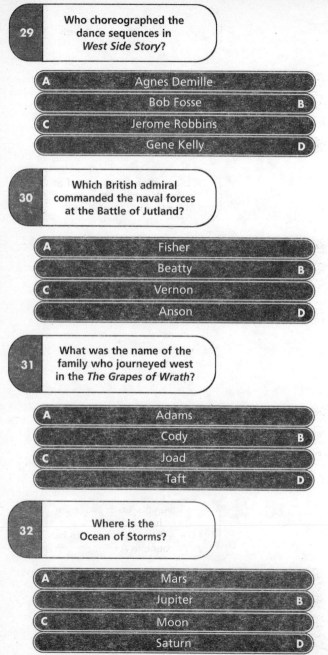

29 Who choreographed the dance sequences in *West Side Story*?

A Agnes Demille

Bob Fosse B

C Jerome Robbins

Gene Kelly D

30 Which British admiral commanded the naval forces at the Battle of Jutland?

A Fisher

Beatty B

C Vernon

Anson D

31 What was the name of the family who journeyed west in the *The Grapes of Wrath*?

A Adams

Cody B

C Joad

Taft D

32 Where is the Ocean of Storms?

A Mars

Jupiter B

C Moon

Saturn D

33 'Rive Gauche' is a famous scent made by which French fashion house?

- **A** Chanel
- **B** Yves St Laurent
- **C** Givenchy
- **D** Cardin

34 A Leopard's head as part of a hallmark denotes the assay office in which British city?

- **A** Birmingham
- **B** Edinburgh
- **C** London
- **D** Sheffield

35 Who was the main female character in the novel *Far From the Madding Crowd*?

- **A** Bathsheba Everdene
- **B** Agnes Grey
- **C** Catherine Earnshaw
- **D** Sophia Western

36 'Give me your tired, your poor, your huddled masses...'. Where is this inscription to be found in America?

- **A** Jefferson Memorial
- **B** Golden Gate Bridge
- **C** Statue of Liberty
- **D** Liberty Bell, Philadelphia

37 What is the name of the heroine of two operas by Puccini and Massenet respectively, based on a story by the Abbe Prevost?

- **A** Thais
- **B** Mimi
- **C** Magda
- **D** Manon

38 What is the common name for Bursitis?

- **A** Tennis elbow
- **B** Housemaid's knee
- **C** Frozen shoulder
- **D** Athlete's foot

39 What punishment was meted out to Abelard after the discovery of his love affair with Heloise?

- **A** Banishment
- **B** Hanging
- **C** Castration
- **D** Torture on the rack

40 Who or what is the Old Man of Hoy?

- **A** Prophet
- **B** Giant pike
- **C** Rock
- **D** Wizard

Le Notre was responsible for designing the gardens of which palace? 41

A Versailles

Buckingham B

C Blenheim

Tuileries D

With which field of fashion design is Emma Hope associated? 42

A Shoes

Jewellery B

C Hats

Knitwear D

Dorothea Brooke is the heroine of which novel? 43

A *Clayhanger*

Vanity Fair B

C *Middlemarch*

A Passage to India D

'One swallow does not a summer make.' Whose saying is this? 44

A Aristophanes

Aristotle B

C Keats

Peter Scott D

45 Vientiane is the capital of which country?

A	Laos	
B	Lithuania	B
C	Lebanon	
D	Lesotho	D

46 Who was Britain's last heavy-weight world boxing champion before Lennox Lewis?

A	Bob Fitzsimmons	
	Frank Bruno	B
C	Henry Cooper	
	Joe Bugner	D

47 What do children learn through the use of the Susuki method?

A	Etiquette	
	Reading	B
C	Riding	
	Violin	D

48 Who was the mother of the Blessed Virgin Mary?

A	St Elizabeth	
	St Anne	B
C	St Cecilia	
	St Helena	D

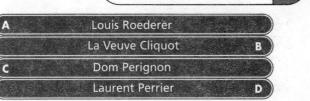

The discovery of the method of making champagne sparkle was attributed to whom?

49

A	Louis Roederer
B	La Veuve Cliquot
C	Dom Perignon
D	Laurent Perrier

'Nemo me impune lacessit' is the motto of which Order of Chivalry?

50

A	Bath
B	Garter
C	Golden Fleece
D	Thistle

Which poet was expelled from both Eton and Oxford?

51

A	Shelley
B	Siegfried Sassoon
C	Byron
D	G K Chesterton

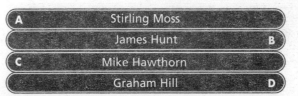

Which driver was the first Briton to become world champion, back in 1958?

52

A	Stirling Moss
B	James Hunt
C	Mike Hawthorn
D	Graham Hill

53 Which of the following was a renowned French cabinetmaker?

A Riesener

Danton B

C Robespierre

Giscard d'Estaing D

54 What is fluoxetine hydrochloride better known as?

A Aspirin

Prozac B

C Viagra

Insulin D

55 Which novel concludes Anthony Powell's series, *A Dance To the Music of Time*?

A *A Question of Upbringing*

The Valley of Bones B

C *Hearing Secret Harmonies*

Casanova's Chinese Restaurant D

56 If you suffered from Prosopagnosia what would you be unable to remember?

A Your lines

Faces B

C Dates

Your way about D

Which playwright wrote two plays designed to be performed simultaneously by the same cast?

57

A	Eugene O'Neill
B	Bertolt Brecht
C	Alan Ayckbourn
D	Ray Cooney

What was the name of Kathleen Hale's most famous character?

58

A	Leander
B	Orlando
C	Felix
D	Valentine

Augustus Melmotte is a character in which of Trollope's novels?

59

A	The Three Clerks
B	The Eustace Diamonds
C	The Way We Live Now
D	Framley Parsonage

Which novel did Charles Dickens leave unfinished when he died?

60

A	A Tale of Two Cities
B	Barnaby Rudge
C	The Cricket on the Hearth
D	The Mystery of Edwin Drood

61 The character of Anthony Blanche in *Brideshead Revisited* was allegedly modelled on which real life person?

A   Oscar Wilde

Aubrey Beardsley   B

C   Harold Acton

John Sutro   D

62 Who is Dona Lucia d'Alvadores more familiarly known as?

A   The Bald Prima Donna

Blithe Spirit   B

C   Charley's Aunt

Our Lady of the Flower   D

63 Amharic is a language spoken in which country?

A   Ethiopia

Syria   B

C   Congo

Tibet   D

64 Which novelist had a son by H G Wells?

A   Rosamond Lehmann

Mrs Gaskell   B

C   Rebecca West

George Eliot   D

The pheasant shooting season begins on which date? 65

A 31 October

12 August B

C 1 September

1 October D

Kabbalah is the mystical tradition of which religion? 66

A Islam

Judaism B

C Taoism

Jainism D

Skopje is the capital of which country? 67

A Madagascar

Malawi B

C Malaysia

Macedonia D

Which famous entrepreneur headed the Australian syndicate when they won yachting's America's Cup in 1983? 68

A Kerry Packer

Rupert Murdoch B

C Alan Bond

Rolf Harris D

69 Zeno of Citium founded which Greek school of philosophers?

A   Epicurians

Cynics   B

C   Stoics

Sceptics   D

70 Which of these conifers does not drop its leaves in winter?

A   Maidenhair Tree

Swamp Cypress   B

C   Dawn Redwood

Deodar   D

71 Which futuristic architect designed the Jewish Museum in Berlin?

A   Nicholas Grimshaw

Zaha Hadid   B

C   Daniel Libeskind

Frank Gehry   D

72 Which French born ballet master and choreographer is credited with the development of Russian classical ballet?

A   Balanchine

Petipa   B

C   Diaghilev

Massine   D

What is the common name for Zantedeschia aethiopica? 73

A Arum lily

Madonna lily B

C Lily of the Valley

Foxtail lily D

Which of these men was a famous pirate in the seventeenth Century? 74

A John Pierpoint Morgan

Sir Henry Morgan B

C Cliff Morgan

William de Morgan D

What is the mathematical equivalent of dyslexia? 75

A Dysarthria

Disgraphia B

C Dyscalculia

Dyskinensis D

Which French author wrote *The Plague*? 76

A Albert Camus

Jean Paul Sartre B

C Jean Cocteau

Marguerite Duras D

77 Which composer wrote 'On Wenlock Edge', a song cycle based on texts from A E Housman's poem 'A Shropshire Lad'?

A Ralph Vaughan Williams

Frederick Delius B

C Edward Elgar

Gustav Holst D

78 Angkor Wat is a twelfth century Hindu temple in which country?

A Cambodia

Thailand B

C Vietnam

Laos D

79 What are baby kangaroos known as?

A Billy

Barry B

C Joey

Wally D

80 Which of the following actors was once also manager of the Theatre Royal, Drury Lane?

A David Garrick

Henry Irving B

C Edmund Kean

John Gielgud D

Which of these countries is the oldest independent republic in Africa? 81

A South Africa
Liberia B
C Mali
Congo D

A quintillion is a one followed by how many noughts? 82

A Twenty
Twenty-five B
C Thirty
Forty D

In a new-born baby, the Moro reflex is another name for which reflex? 83

A Sucking
Startle B
C Grasping
Rooting D

Cartoons for seven tapestries originally intended to be hung in the Sistine Chapel now in the V & A Museum are by which painter? 84

A Michaelangelo
da Vinci B
C Raphael
Caravaggio D

85 In which sport do the Leander club compete?

A Polo

Tennis B

C Rowing

Squash D

86 The poem 'Hugh Selwyn Moberley' was written by which poet?

A Ezra Pound

T S Eliot B

C Richard Aldington

Edith Sitwell D

87 What kind of a voice does the opera singer Sherrill Milnes have?

A Soprano

Contralto B

C Tenor

Baritone D

88 In which city can the Fitzwilliam Museum be found?

A Oxford

Cambridge B

C Manchester

Glasgow D

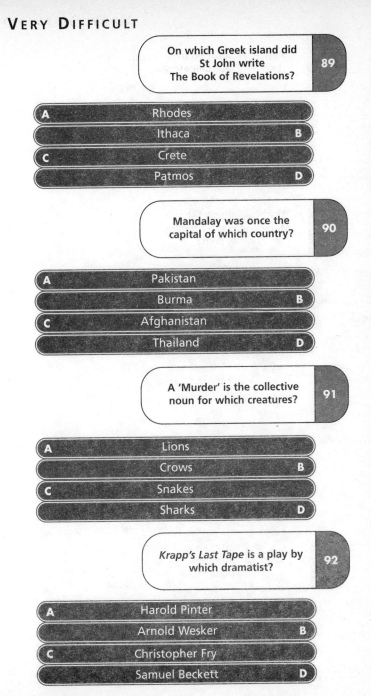

On which Greek island did
St John write
The Book of Revelations?

89

A Rhodes

Ithaca B

C Crete

Patmos D

Mandalay was once the
capital of which country?

90

A Pakistan

Burma B

C Afghanistan

Thailand D

A 'Murder' is the collective
noun for which creatures?

91

A Lions

Crows B

C Snakes

Sharks D

Krapp's Last Tape is a play by
which dramatist?

92

A Harold Pinter

Arnold Wesker B

C Christopher Fry

Samuel Beckett D

93 What does the TT in the Isle of Man TT motorcycling races stand for?

A Triumph Trophy

Tourist Tournament B

C Tourist Trophy

Twisty Track D

94 'A little learning is a dangerous thing;/ Drink deep or taste not the Pierian spring' Who wrote these lines?

A John Milton

Alexander Pope B

C Horace Walpole

John Donne D

95 Henry Kissinger once made an appearance in which TV series?

A Star Trek

Fame B

C Dallas

Dynasty D

96 Dick Diver is the main character in which of Scott Fitzgerald's novels?

A The Great Gatsby

Tender is the Night B

C The Diamond as Big as the Ritz

The Beautiful and the Damned D

97 Paul Storr was renowned as a craftsman in which field of the decorative arts?

A Silver

B Furniture

C Silk weaving

D Tapestry

98 What is buckminsterfullerene?

A Clerical garment

B Form of carbon

C Deer herder

D Monk

99 The Aga Khan is the leader of which sect of Muslims?

A Sunni

B Shiite

C Sufi

D Nizari

100 At which other sport has Test cricketer Everton Weekes represented Barbados?

A Bridge

B Golf

C Darts

D Croquet

101 Bip was the name of a character devised by which performer?

A   Kenny Everett

    Marcel Marceau   B

C   Robin Williams

    Spike Milligan   D

102 Which of the following terms means the outer layer of the skin?

A   Cutis vera

    Epidermis   B

C   Dermis

    Corium   D

103 Who choreographed the American ballet *Appalachian Spring*?

A   Isadora Duncan

    Balanchine   B

C   Jerome Robbins

    Martha Graham   D

104 Which word did Freud use to mean the conscious mind?

A   Id

    Ego   B

C   Libido

    Superego   D

King Ludwig II of Bavaria was the patron of which composer?

105

A — Bruckner

Wagner — **B**

C — Mozart

Brahms — **D**

What was Inspector Morse's christian name?

106

A — Temperance

Endeavour — **B**

C — Venture

Fortitude — **D**

Epidemic Parotitis is the medical name of which common disease?

107

A — Mumps

Measles — **B**

C — Chicken pox

Scarlet fever — **D**

With which Italian city was the Gonzaga family associated?

108

A — Florence

Milan — **B**

C — Padua

Mantua — **D**

109 According to legend, which saint wiped the sweat from Jesus' brow with her veil on the road to Calvary?

A St Mary Magdalene

St Veronica B

C St Martha

St Catherine D

110 Which idea was put forward by James Lovelock?

A Gaia

Global warming B

C Ozone depletion

Climate flips D

111 In John Osborne's play *Look Back in Anger* what was the name of the angry young man hero?

A Johnny Carter

Billy Liar B

C Jimmy Porter

Joe Lampton D

112 The Dayaks are native to which island?

A Borneo

Papua New Guinea B

C Tahiti

Hawaii D

Who gave the cacao plant the Latin name *Theobroma cacao*, meaning 'drink of the gods'?

113

A	Sir Hans Sloane
	Montezuma **B**
C	Linnaeus
	Cadbury **D**

What was the name of the Prussian dynasty that ended with Kaiser Wilhelm?

114

A	Hohenstaufen
	Hapsburg **B**
C	Hohenzollern
	Wittelsbach **D**

Willie Loman is the main protagonist of which of Arthur Miller's plays?

115

A	*After the Fall*
	Death of a Salesman **B**
C	*The Misfits*
	A View from the Bridge **D**

In which sport is the Melbourne Cup contested?

116

A	Yachting
	Cricket **B**
C	Aussie Rules Football
	Horse Racing **D**

117 Who first mixed space and time to come up with four dimensional spacetime?

A Stephen Hawking

B Albert Einstein

C Herman Minkowski

D Richard Feynman

118 Who succeeded in building a replica of Shakespeare's Globe Theatre near its original site in London?

A Sam Wanamaker

B Peter Hall

C Adrian Noble

D Cameron Mackintosh

119 Which bird's call sounds like 'G' back, g' back, g' back'?

A Pheasant

B Grouse

C Starling

D Jackdaw

120 Which musical was based on Thornton Wilder's play *The Matchmaker*?

A *Anything Goes*

B *Hello Dolly*

C *Aspects of Love*

D *Fiddler on the Roof*

Rodrigo Diaz de Vivar, Spanish soldier of fortune, is better known in history by which title? 121

A   Don Quixote

El Cid   B

C   Duke of Alva

El Cordobes   D

In Greece, which mountain is sacred to Apollo? 122

A   Mount Athos

Mount Olympus   B

C   Mount Parnassus

Mount Pelion   D

Who wrote the tune of the hymn 'Onward Christian Soldiers'? 123

A   Sir Edward Elgar

Sir Arthur Sullivan   B

C   Thomas Arne

Dame Ethyl Smyth   D

Greenland is ruled by which country? 124

A   Denmark

Iceland   B

C   Norway

Sweden   D

125 What is a comedo more commonly known as?

A Italian comedian

Blackhead B

C Chamber pot

Cleaning lady D

126 Which Queen did Katharine Hepburn play in *Lion in Winter*?

A Elizabeth of Bohemia

Mary, Queen of Scots B

C Eleanor of Aquitaine

Catherine the Great of Russia D

127 By what name was the revolutionary group who led an uprising in Russia in 1825 known?

A Mensheviks

Decembrists B

C Populists

Girondins D

128 Who presents the Radio 4 programme *The Moral Maze*?

A Peter Sissons

John Humphreys B

C Melvyn Bragg

Michael Buerk D

VERY DIFFICULT

Who quoted Hindu scripture: 'Now I am become death, the destroyer of worlds', when the first atomic bomb was tested?

129

A	Enrico Fermi
B	Otto Hahn
C	Leo Szilard
D	Robert Oppenheimer

In Wagner's *Ring Cycle*, who finally captures the ring forged from the Rhinegold?

130

A	Wotan
B	Siegmund
C	Alberich
D	Brunnhilde

In the sixteenth Century, which architect published his influential 'Quattro Libri dell'Architettura'?

131

A	Alberti
B	Palladio
C	Colen Campbell
D	Vitruvius

Which strait separates North and South Island in New Zealand?

132

A	Darwin
B	Cook
C	Tasman
D	Egmont

133 By what name is a man with a red beard on a green bicycle sometimes known?

A Emperor penguin

Great oyster B

C King Beaver

Fuzzy bear D

134 Which artist made a bronze sculpture of a dancer and dressed her in a muslin skirt and satin hair ribbon?

A Renoir

Maillol B

C Degas

Rodin D

135 David Willcocks was director of which choir from 1960–1998?

A Westminster Abbey

King's College Chapel B

C Bach Choir (London)

Winchester Cathedral D

136 Which football club's away kit was coveted by the band Half Man Half Biscuit?

A Real Madrid

Barcelona B

C Dukla Prague

Dynamo Kiev D

137 Which family lived at the Ponderosa Ranch?

A Clantons

Carringtons B

C Clitheroes

Cartwrights D

138 Bucephalus was the favourite horse of which great military commander?

A Alexander the Great

Napoleon Bonaparte B

C Duke of Wellington

Genghis Khan D

139 *La Regle du Jeu* was which French film director's most famous film?

A Jean Cocteau

Francois Truffaut B

C Rene Clair

Jean Renoir D

140 Which of the following was the name of Rudyard Kipling's house in Sussex?

A Pook's Hill

Batemans B

C Chawton

Dove Cottage D

141 In what 'vehicles' do competitors compete in the Devizes to Westminster Marathon?

A Chariots

Canoes **B**

C Yachts

Rally Cars **D**

142 What was the name of the first Astronomer Royal?

A Isaac Newton

John Flamsteed **B**

C Martin Rees

Edmund Halley **D**

143 Princess Margaret once appeared in an episode of which radio series?

A *Mrs Dale's Diary*

The Glums **B**

C *The Archers*

Life with the Lyons **D**

144 'Stranger in Paradise' is a song from which musical?

A *The King and I*

South Pacific **B**

C *Godspell*

Kismet **D**

Who or what is Rufous Bushchat? 145

- **A** North African bird
- **B** Television presenter
- **C** Derby winner
- **D** Desert fox

In which sport did Andre Agassi's father, Emmanuel, compete for Iran in the 1948 Olympic Games? 146

- **A** Tennis
- **B** Table Tennis
- **C** Boxing
- **D** Badminton

Which opera by Benjamin Britten is based on a story by Herman Melville? 147

- **A** *Albert Herring*
- **B** *Billy Budd*
- **C** *Peter Grimes*
- **D** *Moby Dick*

Who or what is a 'fohn'? 148

- **A** Mountain guide
- **B** Whale
- **C** Wind
- **D** Cheese

149 Which of the following states was not on the Confederate side in the American Civil War?

A New York

Alabama B

C Georgia

Virginia D

150 Who wrote the words of 'Auld Lang Syne'?

A Walter Scott

The Marquis of Montrose B

C Robert Burns

Thomas Mordaunt D

151 Good King Wenceslas was the ruler of which country?

A Hungary

Poland B

C Roumania

Bohemia D

152 Who was the first tight-rope-walker to cross the Niagara Falls?

A Jules Leotard

Philippe Petit B

C Blondin

Houdini D

Who does Hamlet kill while he is hidden behind the arras? `153`

A Yorick

Polonius **B**

C Laertes

Rosencrantz **D.**

What is Occam's Razor? `154`

A The principle of economy

Ancient shaving tool **B**

C A sea bird

A dilemma **D**

What was the name of the sculptor whose figure of Christ temporarily occupied the spare plinth in Trafalgar Square? `155`

A Mark Wallinger

Rachel Whiteread **B**

C Damien Hirst

Barry Flanagan **D**

'Please will you give me a glass of water. I have something in my eye and I want to bathe it.' From which David Lean film? `156`

A Lawrence of Arabia

Dr Zhivago **B**

C Brief Encounter

A Passage to India **D**

157 Which British Prime Minister was responsible for making Queen Victoria Empress of India?

A Gladstone

Disraeli B

C Melbourne

Palmerston D

158 Where in the world is Armageddon?

A Syria

Lebanon B

C Jordan

Israel D

159 Which artist painted the enormous Crucifixion in the Scuola di San Rocco in Venice?

A Giovanni Bellini

Tintoretto B

C Titian

Veronese D

160 Who was Count Laszlo Almasy?

A Tarzan

The Third Man B

C The English Patient

The Hustler D

161 Maudie Littlehampton was a character created by which cartoonist?

A Osbert Lancaster

B Mark Boxer

C Hoffnung

D Nicholas Bentley

162 'Oh for a muse of fire, that would ascend/The brightest heaven of invention' are the first lines of which of Shakespeare's plays?

A Richard III

B Hamlet

C Midsummer Night's Dream

D Henry V

163 In Greek mythology, who was the goddess of the rainbow?

A Iris

B Semele

C Niobe

D Io

164 What kind of an insect is a Downy Emerald?

A Moth

B Butterfly

C Dragonfly

D Grasshopper

165 What was the address of the house in the TV series, *Upstairs, Downstairs*?

A. 165 Eaton Place

B. 129 Kensington Square

C. 459 Bayswater Road

D. 67 Camberwell Green

166 Moral Re-Armament was a Christian revivalist movement begun in the 1930s by whom?

A. Billy Graham

B. John Robinson

C. Frank Buchman

D. Teilhard de Chardin

167 In Ancient Greece, Praxiteles was celebrated in which field?

A. Philosophy

B. Drama

C. Sculpture

D. Mathematics

168 Which member of the royal family includes Earl of Merioneth and Baron Greenwich among his titles?

A. Duke of York

B. Prince of Wales

C. Prince William

D. Duke of Edinburgh

The 'Yellow Hats' are a Buddhist sect from which country?

169

A   Japan

China   B

C   Tibet

India   D

Stephen Wraysford is the hero of which novel?

170

A   *Birdsong*

A Good Man in Africa   B

C   *The Ghost Road*

The Constant Gardener   D

What is the name given to the cyclist at the back of the Tour de France field?

171

A   Tailend Charlie

Le Derriere   B

C   Le Fool

Lantern Rouge   D

Which British medal for gallantry used to be cast from Russian guns captured in the Crimean War?

172

A   George Cross

Military Cross   B

C   Victoria Cross

Distinguished Service Medal   D

173 What is dichlorodiphenyltrichloroethane used for?

A Insecticide

Cough mixture B

C Solvent

Colouring D

174 Who were the Cathars?

A Albigensian heretics

Hungarian aristocrats B

C Scandinavian invaders

Part of the Golden Horde D

175 Which of these great apes names means 'Man of the Forest'?

A Gorilla

Chimpanzee B

C Orang-utan

Siamang D

176 In which of her films did Marilyn Monroe star with Lawrence Olivier?

A Some Like It Hot

The Misfits B

C How to Marry a Millionaire

The Prince and the Showgirl D

The Academy of St Martin-in-the-Fields is a chamber orchestra founded by whom? **177**

A — Roger Norrington

B — Neville Marriner

C — John Eliot Gardiner

D — Simon Rattle

Which event did Britain win at the 1908 Olympics with a team made up of members of the City of London police force? **178**

A — Football

B — Baseball

C — Tug of War

D — Boxing

What is a distinctive feature of a Tuatara? **179**

A — Third eye

B — No tail

C — Black tongue

D — Six toes

From which of T.S. Eliot's *Four Quartets* does the line come 'Human kind/ Cannot bear very much reality'? **180**

A — 'Burnt Norton'

B — 'East Coker'

C — 'The Dry Salvages'

D — 'Little Gidding'

181 Benjamin Britten's *War Requiem* used texts from which British poet's work?

A Siegfried Sassoon

B Rupert Brooke

C Wilfred Owen

D A E Houseman

182 What does an acarologist study?

A Fish

B Mites and ticks

C Gums

D Worms

183 Granta is the Roman name for which English town?

A Grantham

B York

C Cambridge

D Gloucester

184 Who or what is likely to suffer from a Mosaic virus?

A Rabbi

B Plant

C Flooring

D Sheep

In 1960, which city was destroyed by an earthquake? 185

A Aden

Algiers B

C Agadir

Abadan D

'Age cannot wither her, nor custom stale/ Her infinite variety. Of whom was this spoken? 186

A Helen of Troy

Cleopatra B

C Desdemona

Ophelia D

Cape Trafalgar is to be found on which coastline? 187

A Southern Spain

Southern Portugal B

C Southern France

Southern Italy D

Who was the director of the film *Death in Venice*? 188

A Bertolucci

Fellini B

C Visconti

Antonioni D

189 The architect and sculptor Bernini was the greatest exponent of which artistic style?

A High Renaissance

Rococo B

C Neo-Classicism

Baroque D

190 A nemathelminth is a type of which of the following?

A Bird

Plant B

C Worm

Insect D

191 Who or what was Cymbeline?

A Super-model

British tribal chieftain B

C Musical instrument

Legendary country D

192 Where in London is the bronze sculpture of Winston Churchill and Franklin D Roosevelt sitting together on a bench?

A Piccadilly

Grosvenor Square B

C Whitehall

Bond Street D

193 What is the name of the process by which lighter elements 'cook' to form heavier ones in stars?

A Nucleosynthesis

B Fission

C Elementisation

D Nucleating

194 In the Wilton Diptych which king of England is depicted being presented to the Virgin and Child by his patron saints?

A William the Conqueror

B Richard Coeur de Lion

C Richard II

D Henry VIII

195 In Jung's thinking, which word describes the inner, unconscious feminine side of a man?

A Anima

B Animus

C Eros

D Logos

196 In which film did Fred Astaire dance with Cyd Charisse?

A Top Hat

B Flying Down to Rio

C Swing Time

D Silk Stockings

197 Which mathematician is often called the father of artificial intelligence?

A   Alan Turing

   Clive Sinclair   B

C   Marvin Minsky

   David Hilbert   D

198 Where would the Islets of Langerhans be found?

A   Scotland

   Pancreas   B

C   Fish Restaurant

   Moon   D

199 Which is the former name of Belize?

A   British Honduras

   Spanish Guinea   B

C   Guatemala

   San Salvador   D

200 Who is married to cricketer Alec Stewart's sister?

A   Graeme Thorpe

   Mark Butcher   B

C   Alan Lamb

   Angus Fraser   D

Answers

Easy

1	**C**	Madonna
2	**C**	Plate tectonics
3	**B**	Mayflower
4	**A**	St Nicholas
5	**B**	The Cavern
6	**D**	Rabbits
7	**B**	Thunder
8	**A**	Yew
9	**C**	Jeanne d'Arc
10	**A**	Coffee
11	**C**	Sleeplessness
12	**C**	Spider
13	**C**	Tortoise
14	**C**	*Romeo and Juliet*
15	**A**	Architecture
16	**B**	Stubbs
17	**A**	Elephant
18	**B**	Canute
19	**C**	Nana
20	**B**	Wren
21	**B**	Potomac
22	**B**	Distemper
23	**B**	Pit
24	**C**	Pumpkin
25	**C**	Docking
26	**A**	Cape of Good Hope
27	**A**	A unit of energy
28	**C**	Tom
29	**C**	St Christopher
30	**D**	Fortune telling
31	**C**	Marx
32	**C**	Olympus
33	**C**	French
34	**A**	Restart it
35	**C**	Carbohydrate
36	**B**	Toulouse Lautrec
37	**B**	Noel Coward
38	**C**	Athens
39	**B**	Tracy Emin
40	**D**	Diabetes
41	**B**	Gibraltar
42	**C**	Counting rings
43	**B**	Moses
44	**A**	Druids

45	**B**	Sagittarius
46	**A**	The view from Westminster Bridge
47	**D**	Albatross
48	**C**	Waltzes
49	**C**	Tweed
50	**C**	Gold
51	**B**	Malta
52	**B**	Primrose
53	**C**	603
54	**C**	Two dancers
55	**B**	Siamese
56	**C**	South Florida,USA
57	**C**	Stanley
58	**C**	William the Conqueror
59	**A**	Letter from America
60	**A**	John Betjeman
61	**A**	Peak in Northern Ireland
62	**C**	Fishing
63	**A**	Sahara
64	**D**	Pessimism
65	**B**	Bo
66	**D**	Heel
67	**B**	Michael Jackson
68	**C**	Chequers
69	**C**	Cardigan
70	**D**	Coliseum
71	**B**	*MASH*
72	**C**	George Washington
73	**A**	World War I
74	**B**	Alfred the Great
75	**B**	Mount Ararat
76	**B**	Opera
77	**B**	Napoleon
78	**A**	Flower
79	**C**	Endeavour
80	**C**	Royal Academy of Dramatic Arts
81	**B**	Cavaliers
82	**C**	Dallas
83	**A**	Alexander Graham Bell
84	**B**	Pooh and Piglet
85	**D**	Ten
86	**C**	Normandy
87	**B**	David Niven

88	**B**	Hardy	139	**D**	Toes
89	**C**	Sir Richard Whittington	140	**C**	Roof
90	**D**	Chile	141	**B**	Lewis Carroll
91	**B**	Anno Domini	142	**D**	The Albatross
92	**C**	Malaysia	143	**C**	Atlas
93	**B**	Molten rock	144	**D**	Quentin Crisp
94	**C**	Ukraine	145	**B**	Light
95	**B**	Twister	146	**C**	Have a drink
96	**C**	The Diet of Worms	147	**B**	1972
97	**B**	Lions	148	**B**	Westminster Abbey
98	**C**	Pennines	149	**B**	Tate Modern
99	**A**	Bonnie Prince Charlie	150	**B**	Horse Chestnut
100	**C**	1953	151	**C**	Darling
101	**B**	Patience	152	**A**	Sunderland
102	**C**	Russell Crowe	153	**B**	Cinderella
103	**B**	Lamb	154	**D**	Norman Mailer
104	**C**	USA	155	**D**	Germaine Greer
105	**A**	Seat	156	**C**	High Jump
106	**B**	Christian Dior	157	**D**	*Lady Chatterley's Lover*
107	**D**	Italy	158	**C**	Cuba Libre
108	**A**	Music Hall	159	**C**	Ferrari
109	**B**	Counters	160	**C**	Hallow'een
110	**D**	Goliath	161	**D**	Prince of Wales feathers
111	**D**	Peas	162	**A**	Windsor
112	**D**	Rornmel	163	**D**	The Body Shop
113	**A**	The Charge of the Light Brigade	164	**B**	Broth
114	**B**	Julius Caesar	165	**A**	Gryffindor
115	**C**	Gorbachev	166	**B**	Zephyr
116	**C**	Jamie Oliver	167	**D**	Cello
117	**C**	Supermodel	168	**C**	Monet
118	**C**	Still Life	169	**B**	Plants
119	**B**	Shoes	170	**C**	Valentina Tereshkova
120	**C**	Yorkshire	171	**A**	Fish
121	**B**	Hedwig	172	**A**	Aldermaston
122	**A**	SAS	173	**C**	Van Gogh
123	**D**	Shere Khan	174	**D**	Chip
124	**C**	Geoff Hurst	175	**D**	Florence
125	**D**	Gulf Stream	176	**A**	Television
126	**C**	Beth	177	**B**	David Bailey
127	**A**	Sir Percy Blakeney	178	**C**	Crash
128	**D**	Bilbo Baggins	179	**C**	Bronze
129	**B**	Arthur Miller	180	**A**	Archimedes
130	**B**	Tiffany's	181	**D**	Mercury
131	**B**	Twenty thousand	182	**B**	Measures radioactivity
132	**C**	Katherina	183	**C**	Samuel Johnson
133	**C**	Michigan	184	**D**	Hydrogen
134	**B**	Aramaic	185	**C**	One that is mostly inert
135	**C**	Woodstock	186	**C**	Canaan
136	**C**	Impressionism	187	**B**	Bacteria
137	**A**	The Bank of England	188	**C**	Samuel Pepys
138	**B**	Augustus	189	**A**	Turner

190	**A**	Sea
191	**D**	Read it
192	**D**	Canterbury
193	**C**	Novelist
194	**C**	Dick Francis
195	**A**	Carbon
196	**C**	III
197	**B**	A collection of stars
198	**C**	Viruses
199	**D**	Teeth
200	**B**	Photosynthesis
201	**B**	Brookside
202	**B**	*Snatch*
203	**C**	Tamzin Outhwaite
204	**A**	Iris
205	**B**	*Thriller*
206	**C**	Madonna
207	**B**	Duke Nukem
208	**B**	Vivien Leigh
209	**C**	Wham!
210	**B**	Falcon
211	**D**	Tipsy
212	**B**	Going down
213	**C**	Spike
214	**A**	San Andreas
215	**D**	Bluto
216	**C**	*Toy Story*
217	**B**	Elizabeth Taylor
218	**B**	Crystal Palace
219	**C**	Tchaikovsky
220	**B**	Christopher Cockerell
221	**D**	Isadora Duncan
222	**D**	Robin Hood
223	**B**	Luciano Pavarotti
224	**A**	Jamaica
225	**C**	Wagner
226	**C**	Bass
227	**D**	Hungary
228	**D**	T S Eliot
229	**C**	Prince Regent
230	**C**	Bayeux
231	**C**	G B Shaw
232	**D**	Baseball
233	**C**	Catherine Parr
234	**D**	Roy Tucker
235	**A**	Pembrokeshire corgi
236	**D**	Bud Flanagan
237	**B**	Guy Fawkes
238	**C**	John Peel
239	**C**	US Masters
240	**B**	Kiwi

241	**B**	Nile
242	**C**	*Today*
243	**C**	Harry Houdini
244	**B**	Alan Freeman
245	**A**	Apple
246	**D**	Mime artist
247	**B**	Spain
248	**D**	Trumpet
249	**B**	Theocracy
250	**B**	Elvis Presley
251	**B**	Hastings
252	**C**	*The Mousetrap*
253	**D**	*Macbeth*
254	**B**	Nicholas II
255	**D**	Gods
256	**C**	Christopher Columbus
257	**D**	Bach
258	**A**	Adam's Apple
259	**B**	Aurora australis
260	**C**	Richter scale
261	**B**	'Blue Moon'
262	**A**	Sausage
263	**A**	Rosinante
264	**D**	Bill Shankly
265	**B**	Monkeys
266	**B**	Flanders
267	**C**	Chris Waddle
268	**D**	Peter O'Toole
269	**C**	Bridge
270	**D**	The bails
271	**C**	Giant Panda
272	**C**	1960
273	**C**	SW19
274	**B**	Taiga
275	**A**	Willow
276	**D**	Dock leaf
277	**A**	Bolero
278	**C**	Joseph
279	**C**	Italy
280	**A**	Mrs Malaprop
281	**C**	St Patrick
282	**B**	Roger Bannister
283	**C**	Pianissimo
284	**D**	Harmonica
285	**D**	New York
286	**C**	Esmeralda
287	**A**	Beethoven
288	**D**	John Travolta
289	**B**	*The King and I*
290	**C**	Louvre Museum, Paris
291	**B**	Damien Hirst

292	**D**	*The Prophet*
293	**A**	Michaelangelo
294	**C**	John le Carre
295	**B**	Charles Ryder
296	**B**	Sir Christopher Wren
297	**A**	Black
298	**D**	Rudolph Nureyev
299	**B**	Sieve
300	**B**	Window
301	**D**	Eros
302	**C**	Rudyard Kipling
303	**D**	Dougal
304	**D**	Stucco
305	**A**	Wind
306	**C**	Trafalgar Square
307	**B**	Cerebellum
308	**C**	Arthur
309	**A**	Sow's ear
310	**D**	Coventry
311	**D**	Aga sagas
312	**C**	Mont Blanc
313	**A**	Springfield Elementary
314	**B**	Golden
315	**A**	Sue Lawley
316	**B**	Fred Perry
317	**C**	Spice Girls
318	**A**	Elizabeth David

319	**A**	Five
320	**C**	Jonah
321	**C**	Cardiff City
322	**C**	Kalahari
323	**B**	John Buchan
324	**B**	A duck
325	**C**	Sparrow
326	**B**	*Manderley*
327	**C**	East Africa
328	**A**	Quinquereme of Nineveh
329	**B**	Evelyn Waugh
330	**A**	John Lennon
331	**A**	Patrick Leigh Fermor
332	**B**	Teetotal
333	**A**	William Rufus
334	**B**	Madame de Pompadour
335	**B**	A developing insect
336	**A**	An Asian tent
337	**B**	Warren Beatty
338	**B**	*Robinson Crusoe*
339	**A**	Short sightedness
340	**A**	Rain for six weeks after
341	**D**	Queens Park Rangers
342	**B**	Wildebeest
343	**B**	A baby born feet first
344	**B**	Parsnips

Tricky

1	**C**	Ear
2	**C**	Ostrich
3	**B**	Traffic
4	**B**	Horse
5	**B**	Chekov
6	**B**	Bat
7	**C**	Mulberry
8	**C**	Elsa
9	**B**	Lodge
10	**C**	Crayfish
11	**B**	Hercules
12	**B**	Dream Works
13	**C**	Albatross
14	**B**	Marcel

15	**C**	School
16	**C**	Albert Finney
17	**C**	Matt Damon
18	**B**	E4
19	**A**	La Scala
20	**B**	Robbie Williams
21	**B**	Alan Ball
22	**B**	Arsenal
23	**D**	Norfolk
24	**D**	Dave Beasant
25	**C**	Typhoon
26	**C**	Madeira
27	**C**	Shropshire
28	**D**	Billabong

29	**B**	Copenhagen
30	**B**	Donald Bradman
31	**A**	Apsley House
32	**C**	Archipelago
33	**B**	Seven
34	**A**	Mediterranean
35	**C**	Tatler
36	**B**	Sam Goldwyn
37	**B**	Gladstone
38	**D**	Hamlet
39	**B**	April's there
40	**C**	Vienna
41	**C**	Nevermore
42	**C**	Croquet mallets
43	**D**	Weaver
44	**A**	Vita Sackville West
45	**B**	South Africa
46	**C**	Jupiter
47	**A**	*As You Like It*
48	**B**	*The Cherry Orchard*
49	**A**	Eugene O'Neill
50	**A**	*Martin Chuzzlewitt*
51	**B**	Convict
52	**C**	Tiger
53	**B**	P D James
54	**C**	Water of life
55	**B**	Olympic Games
56	**C**	Pavlova
57	**B**	Sherry
58	**D**	Mayfair
59	**C**	Poker
60	**A**	Shrove Tuesday
61	**D**	Robert Baden Powell
62	**B**	Ruby
63	**B**	Porcelain
64	**B**	Ferdinand
65	**A**	Bordeaux
66	**C**	Protractor
67	**D**	Marengo
68	**C**	Base
69	**A**	Benjamin Franklin
70	**B**	Dialysis
71	**A**	Venus
72	**A**	A solar cell
73	**A**	Cryonics
74	**D**	Mormons
75	**C**	Dolly Parton
76	**C**	Sir Edward Elgar
77	**C**	Fly-by-wire
78	**B**	Mecca
79	**A**	Duke of Medina Sidonia
80	**C**	Daniel
81	**B**	microbes
82	**C**	Nostradamus
83	**C**	Midas
84	**B**	Cryptozoology
85	**C**	Winged horse
86	**C**	Norway
87	**A**	Esau
88	**A**	Wine
89	**C**	St Paul
90	**B**	1919
91	**B**	Hans Holbein
92	**C**	Franklin Delano Roosevelt
93	**D**	Malplaquet
94	**B**	Louis XVI
95	**C**	Hungary
96	**B**	Joshua
97	**C**	Boer War
98	**B**	Crystal Palace
99	**B**	Birds
100	**C**	Edouard Munch
101	**D**	Lord Mountbatten
102	**D**	Velasquez
103	**C**	Anthony Gormley
104	**B**	Fish
105	**C**	Michaelangelo
106	**C**	Norman
107	**C**	Woodcarver
108	**C**	Sergei Diaghilev
109	**B**	Spider
110	**C**	Ruminant
111	**C**	Agoraphobia
112	**C**	Skin
113	**D**	Moccasin
114	**A**	Sir Edwin Landseer
115	**B**	King Edward
116	**C**	Eel
117	**D**	Muscular
118	**A**	Sunflowers
119	**C**	Foxglove
120	**D**	Horse Chestnut
121	**C**	Cuckoo
122	**D**	Nigel Hawthorne
123	**C**	Sailors
124	**C**	Swimming
125	**D**	Stephen Sondheim
126	**B**	*South Pacific*
127	**C**	*Guys and Dolls*
128	**C**	Crane fly
129	**C**	Sue Ellen
130	**B**	Edward Fox
131	**C**	Mozart
132	**C**	Nine

133	**B**	Marquess of Queensbury
134	**B**	Vienna
135	**C**	Bob Beamon
136	**B**	Douglas Jardine
137	**B**	Vesuvius
138	**A**	Scotland
139	**A**	Yuri Gagarin
140	**B**	White Sea
141	**A**	Abacus
142	**B**	Estonia
143	**A**	Sky
144	**C**	Chrysanthemum
145	**B**	Edinburgh
146	**D**	Detroit
147	**B**	Henry Ford
148	**B**	Seven
149	**B**	North Sea
150	**D**	Quaver
151	**B**	Wind
152	**C**	Louise Brown
153	**B**	Athens
154	**C**	International Space Station
155	**D**	Star
156	**B**	Sodium hydroxide
157	**C**	The Bahamas
158	**D**	Solidarity
159	**C**	Fletcher Christian
160	**B**	Nasser
161	**C**	Rasputin
162	**C**	Little Big Horn
163	**A**	Crete
164	**B**	Robben Island
165	**C**	Aristotle
166	**C**	Richard III
167	**C**	St Helena
168	**C**	Cleopatra
169	**A**	Nicaragua
170	**B**	Louis XIV
171	**B**	Casting bronzes
172	**D**	John Vanbrugh
173	**C**	Frank Lloyd Wright
174	**C**	St Petersburg
175	**C**	Pre-Raphaelite Brotherhood
176	**D**	Quentin Tarantino
177	**C**	Impasto
178	**C**	Cary Grant
179	**B**	Gerald Scarfe
180	**C**	E H Shepard
181	**A**	Iceni
182	**B**	Minim
183	**D**	Tchaikovsky

184	**C**	Grey Gables
185	**C**	Jack and Rose
186	**B**	Man Ray
187	**B**	Michaelangelo
188	**D**	Fresco
189	**A**	Drury Lane
190	**C**	Maria Callas
191	**B**	*La Boheme*
192	**C**	Savoy
193	**B**	Johann Strauss
194	**C**	*My Fair Lady*
195	**B**	*Sunset Boulevard*
196	**A**	10
197	**D**	Steptoe and Son
198	**A**	David Frost
199	**B**	Cat and Fiddle
200	**C**	Lord Reith
201	**A**	Butterfly
202	**A**	Virgin
203	**D**	Emperor
204	**D**	West Indies
205	**B**	Wimbledon Ladies' Singles Champion
206	**C**	Gracie Fields
207	**B**	Gold Rings
208	**B**	Bob Dylan
209	**B**	Simon and Garfunkel
210	**B**	Comets
211	**B**	Clifton Suspension Bridge
212	**D**	Monaco
213	**C**	Joe Davis
214	**C**	Classic FM
215	**C**	Showjumping
216	**C**	*Show Boat*
217	C	22
218	**C**	Aldeburgh
219	**D**	Guitar
220	**C**	Berwick Rangers
221	**D**	William Webb Ellis
222	**A**	California
223	**A**	Ionian
224	**D**	'The House of the Rising Sun'
225	**B**	A musical Instrument
226	**C**	Laugharne
227	**C**	Tom Wolfe
228	**D**	Giotto
229	**A**	A portal to the heart
230	**A**	Maggie Tulliver
231	**A**	Matthew Kneale
232	**C**	Volga

Hard

1	D	Wind Instrument
2	C	Yugoslavia
3	C	Dalmation
4	C	Danny Blanchflower
5	A	Hertfordshire
6	B	Earl of Moray
7	C	Shoulder
8	B	George Eliot
9	C	*Crime and Punishment*
10	B	Belshazzar's feast
11	A	Two
12	C	Dragonfly
13	C	Barabbas
14	B	Cat
15	A	Bathymetry
16	A	ER
17	C	Narcissus
18	C	Boating Song
19	D	Gielgud
20	C	Doge
21	C	Henrik Ibsen
22	C	Mr Universe
23	B	Seurat
24	C	*Butterfield Eight*
25	C	Hoof
26	B	Mammal
27	D	Big Daddy
28	B	Placido Domingo
29	C	Citronella
30	B	Pushkin
31	B	*Don Quixote*
32	C	Hugh Laurie
33	C	Venezuela
34	B	Chris Blackwell
35	C	Mozart
36	C	Let the buyer beware
37	D	Garrincha
38	B	Byron
39	D	Greg Norman
40	A	Werner Heisenberg
41	D	Massachusetts
42	A	Jean Foucault
43	C	La Manche
44	B	Cleveland
45	B	Arno
46	C	Antelope
47	D	Istanbul
48	C	Palindrome
49	B	Pacific
50	C	Ninette de Valois
51	C	*The Water Babies*
52	B	American Samoa
53	C	Beaufort
54	C	Petra
55	C	Bayreuth
56	A	Tagus
57	C	*The Merchant of Venice*
58	C	Monegasque
59	B	Montgolfier
60	D	Lord Curzon
61	A	Akenfield
62	D	Hands
63	B	Maigret
64	C	Red Herring
65	C	California
66	D	The Rev William Spooner
67	C	Far to go
68	D	Verdi
69	D	The Press
70	B	Blackcurrant
71	A	Rudyard Kipling
72	B	King Cobra
73	B	Ashley Wilkes
74	A	Grand Canal, China
75	B	Montmorency
76	C	Kenneth Clark
77	D	Edward Albee
78	A	In pastry
79	C	*The Tempest*
80	B	Ass
81	B	Shetlands
82	A	*Under Milk Wood*
83	B	Edith Wharton
84	B	Risotto
85	B	Eat it
86	B	Natasha
87	C	Methuselah
88	D	Mark Twain
89	C	Stoat
90	D	Nora
91	C	Newmarket
92	C	Knitting

93	D	Fuzzy Logic
94	C	Ithaca
95	D	Jocelyn Bell
96	A	Musth
97	C	Glowing substance in glow-worms
98	B	Beetle
99	C	Bit
100	B	Amino acids
101	B	Y
102	B	Gorilla
103	B	Resistant bacterium
104	A	Lizard
105	C	Dog
106	D	−273.15 °C
107	D	Fish
108	A	New Year
109	B	Virgin maid
110	C	Luke
111	B	Stormy petrels
112	C	Parkinson
113	B	Scientology
114	B	Son
115	C	Harold Pinter
116	C	Aphrodite
117	B	Makes plants grow
118	A	Franco
119	B	Lawrence Olivier
120	B	Elizabeth of Bohemia
121	C	Ethiopia
122	C	Prime Minister
123	B	Lord Byron
124	B	Kittens
125	B	Port Moresby
126	C	Kitchener
127	B	Black September
128	B	Python
129	A	Wat Tyler
130	D	Old Man's Beard
131	B	Norway
132	B	Bird
133	D	John Singer Sargent
134	C	Gloria Swanson
135	B	Barcelona
136	D	Cat Stevens
137	C	Serpentine
138	C	Sir Joshua Reynolds
139	A	*The Wizard of Oz*
140	B	Misericord
141	B	Sea of Marmara
142	B	Vivien Leigh
143	C	Velasquez

144	C	Nerve
145	C	Fountain
146	B	Animal skin
147	B	*Dynasty*
148	C	Monkey
149	C	Edward I
150	C	Mongoose
151	D	Caspian
152	C	Bird
153	B	Leonardo di Caprio
154	B	Beetle
155	C	Sir Robert Peel
156	A	Billie
157	B	Stinkhorn
158	C	H M Bateman
159	C	*Apocalypse Now*
160	D	Attosecond
161	C	Carol Reed
162	C	Michigan
163	D	Stravinsky
164	D	Giotto
165	B	*Aida*
166	B	James 'Buster' Douglas
167	A	Haemophilia
168	C	Edinburgh
169	B	Tigris
170	B	John Donne
171	A	*Tosca*
172	B	Dick Francis
173	B	*High Society*
174	B	Calorimeter
175	B	Nimbostratus
176	C	*Annie Get Your Gun*
177	C	Esha Ness
178	D	*Mastermind*
179	C	Hard paste porcelain
180	B	Bernadotte
181	B	Billy Connolly
182	C	Larkin
183	C	Keats
184	C	Ned Sherrin
185	D	Terry Wogan
186	C	Edward Elgar
187	B	London Philharmonic
188	C	Oboe
189	B	*Die Meistersingers*
190	A	*Madame Butterfly*
191	C	Play it
192	D	Shah Jehan
193	B	Harold Abrahams
194	B	Sonny Bono
195	C	Portrait Miniatures

196	**C**	Vera Lynn		211	**C**	The Lady of Shalott
197	**C**	Ang Lee		212	**A**	Colorado
198	**B**	Charles II		213	**D**	Shooting
199	**C**	Portugal		214	**C**	*Mother Courage*
200	**D**	Krakatoa		215	**C**	Zanzibar
201	**A**	A for Adultery		216	**C**	Matilda
202	**C**	Cairngorm		217	**B**	David Cornwall
203	**D**	Dog		218	**B**	Painting
204	**C**	*Funny Girl*		219	**D**	Newton
205	**B**	Switzerland		220	**A**	Sir Arthur Pinero
206	**C**	David Broome		221	**B**	Charles Babbage
207	**A**	Jan van Eyck		222	**C**	Alec Guinness
208	**C**	E F Benson		223	**D**	Napoleon
209	**B**	Gustave Flaubert		224	**D**	*Hair*
210	**B**	Scunthorpe				

Very Difficult

1	**A**	Johnny Scott		29	**C**	Jerome Robbins
2	**B**	Porphyria		30	**B**	Beatty
3	**C**	Vita Sackville West		31	**C**	Joad
4	**A**	1000 Guineas		32	**C**	Moon
5	**C**	Stamps		33	**B**	Yves St Laurent
6	**C**	Salisbury		34	**C**	London
7	**D**	Ultramarine		35	**A**	Bathsheba Everdene
8	**C**	Nebuchadnezzar		36	**C**	Statue of Liberty
9	**D**	Gipsy Moth IV		37	**D**	Manon
10	**C**	Bonsai		38	**B**	Housemaid's knee
11	**B**	The Nightingale		39	**C**	Castration
12	**C**	*King Lear*		40	**C**	Rock
13	**B**	Algae		41	**A**	Versailles
14	**C**	Hummingbird		42	**A**	Shoes
15	**D**	Russia		43	**C**	*Middlemarch*
16	**A**	Peter Shaffer		44	**B**	Aristotle
17	**C**	*The Oldie*		45	**A**	Laos
18	**B**	Descartes		46	**A**	Bob Fitzsimmons
19	**D**	Brain function		47	**D**	Violin
20	**B**	Arizona		48	**B**	St Anne
21	**A**	Guy de Maupassant		49	**C**	Dom Perignon
22	**C**	Art Nouveau		50	**D**	Thistle
23	**C**	Grace Kelly		51	**A**	Shelley
24	**A**	Robert Lowell		52	**C**	Mike Hawthorn
25	**C**	Anubis		53	**A**	*Riesener*
26	**B**	Cheltenham		54	**B**	Prozac
27	**B**	South Africa		55	**C**	*Hearing Secret Harmonies*
28	**D**	Pushkin		56	**B**	Faces

57	**C**	Alan Ayckbourn
58	**B**	Orlando
59	**C**	*The Way We Live Now*
60	**D**	*The Mystery of Edwin Drood*
61	**C**	Harold Acton
62	**C**	Charley's Aunt
63	**A**	Ethiopia
64	**C**	Rebecca West
65	**D**	1 October
66	**B**	Judaism
67	**D**	Macedonia
68	**C**	Alan Bond
69	**C**	Stoics
70	**D**	Deodar
71	**C**	Daniel Libeskind
72	**B**	Petipa
73	**A**	Arum lily
74	**B**	Sir Henry Morgan
75	**C**	Dyscalculia
76	**A**	Albert Camus
77	**A**	Ralph Vaughan Williams
78	**A**	Cambodia
79	**C**	Joey
80	**A**	David Garrick
81	**B**	Liberia
82	**C**	Thirty
83	**B**	Startle
84	**C**	Raphael
85	**C**	Rowing
86	**A**	Ezra Pound
87	**D**	Baritone
88	**B**	Cambridge
89	**D**	Patmos
90	**B**	Burma
91	**B**	Crows
92	**D**	Samuel Beckett
93	**C**	Tourist Trophy
94	**B**	Alexander Pope
95	**D**	*Dynasty*
96	**B**	*Tender is the Night*
97	**A**	Silver
98	**B**	Form of carbon
99	**D**	Nizari
100	**A**	Bridge
101	**B**	Marcel Marceau
102	**B**	Epidermis
103	**D**	Martha Graham
104	**B**	Ego
105	**B**	Wagner
106	**B**	Endeavour
107	**A**	Mumps

108	**D**	Mantua
109	**B**	St Veronica
110	**A**	Gaia
111	**C**	Jimmy Porter
112	**A**	Borneo
113	**C**	Linnaeus
114	**C**	Hohenzollern
115	**B**	*Death of a Salesman*
116	**D**	Horse Racing
117	**C**	Herman Minkowski
118	**A**	Sam Wanamaker
119	**B**	Grouse
120	**B**	*Hello Dolly*
121	**B**	El Cid
122	**C**	Mount Parnassus
123	**B**	Sir Arthur Sullivan
124	**A**	Denmark
125	**B**	Blackhead
126	**C**	Eleanor of Aquitaine
127	**B**	Decembrists
128	**D**	Michael Buerk
129	**D**	Robert Oppenheimer
130	**D**	Brunnhilde
131	**B**	Palladio
132	**B**	Cook
133	**C**	King beaver
134	**C**	Degas
135	**C**	Bach Choir (London)
136	**C**	Dukla Prague
137	**D**	Cartwrights
138	**A**	Alexander the Great
139	**D**	Jean Renoir
140	**B**	Batemans
141	**B**	Canoes
142	**B**	John Flamsteed
143	**C**	The Archers
144	**D**	*Kismet*
145	**A**	North African bird
146	**C**	Boxing
147	**B**	*Billy Budd*
148	**C**	Wind
149	**A**	New York
150	**C**	Robert Burns
151	**D**	Bohemia
152	**C**	Blondin
153	**B**	Polonius
154	**A**	The principle of economy
155	**A**	Mark Wallinger
156	**C**	*Brief Encounter*
157	**B**	Disraeli
158	**D**	Israel

159	**B**	Tintoretto		180	**A**	'Burnt Norton'
160	**C**	*The English Patient*		181	**C**	Wilfred Owen
161	**A**	Osbert Lancaster		182	**B**	Mites and ticks
162	**D**	*Henry V*		183	**C**	Cambridge
163	**A**	Iris		184	**B**	Plant
164	**C**	Dragonfly		185	**C**	Agadir
165	**A**	165 Eaton Place		186	**B**	Cleopatra
166	**C**	Frank Buchman		187	**A**	Southern Spain
167	**C**	Sculpture		188	**C**	Visconti
168	**D**	Duke of Edinburgh		189	**D**	Baroque
169	**C**	Tibet		190	**C**	Worm
170	**A**	*Birdsong*		191	**B**	British tribal chieftain
171	**D**	Lantern Rouge		192	**D**	Bond Street
172	**C**	Victoria Cross		193	**A**	Nucleosynthesis
173	**A**	Insecticide		194	**C**	Richard II
174	**A**	Albigensian heretics		195	**A**	Anima
175	**C**	Orang-utan		196	**D**	*Silk Stockings*
176	**D**	*The Prince and the Showgirl*		197	**A**	Alan Turing
177	**B**	Neville Marriner		198	**B**	Pancreas
178	**C**	Tug of War		199	**A**	British Honduras
179	**A**	Third eye		200	**B**	Mark Butcher

Hints from Judith

1   Try the Celtic fringe.
2   An hereditary illness sometimes causing mental confusion.
3   One of the two who caused a scandal with their elopement.
4   Go for guineas for girls.
5   At least it is an ecologically sound hobby.
6   Think of the one with the tallest spire or in the most northerly situation.
7   Choose one of the colours from overseas.
8   Eliminate the Persian and Macedonian rulers.
9   This boat had wings!
10 Now then, no fighting or folding.
11 The choice is between two summer residents.
12 Stormy weather.
13 Give no thought to colours or greenery.
14 Choose one of the tropical birds.
15 It is a lake in the very far north.
16 Keep it in the family.
17 Now he is older, maybe he is just content to be a looker-on.
18 Rule out the non-Christians.
19 Greenhouse gases and global warming are linked but they are not the answer.
20 Is it likely to be a northern state?
21 Choose one of the two with pretensions to nobility.
22 Think pre-World War I.
23 Choose between the two who starred in the same film about a wedding sixteen years apart.
24 Ignore the two who were publicly into drugs.
25 Go for the god of the living or the dead.
26 Look at the two racecourses in the south-west.
27 Rule out the European mountains.
28 Rule out the two who each spent years living in other European countries.
29 Choose one of the two men who started out as dancers.
30 Remember that Jutland was a twentieth century battle.
31 Theirs was not a Presidential name.
32 Calm reigns on planets dedicated to the gods of war and the sky.
33 Not one of Coco's or Pierre's.
34 Eliminate cities in the old industrial heartland.

35 Remember that two of these are Bronte heroines.
36 A welcome message at one of the ports on the eastern seaboard.
37 She either expires from TB or from the rigours of a journey into exile.
38 You could get it from serving in court or at home.
39 They made absolutely sure he'd never have another love affair.
40 He is neither a magician nor a clairvoyant.
41 He designed gardens in his native land.
42 Fashionable at top or toe.
43 She was a female writer's heroine.
44 Those ancient Greeks were wise old birds.
45 Sounds as if it might have been a French colony or Protectorate.
46 Rule out two who were definitely too old.
47 They learn to bow and scrape.
48 Eliminate the two saints not mentioned in the New Testament.
49 Try the merry widow or the monk.
50 It is all in the Latin.
51 Think of two who were friends and both died abroad.
52 Choose between the two who both had fatal accidents.
53 Eliminate the revolutionaries.
54 Take your pick between a mental or a physical pain-killer.
55 Choose one of the two with allusions to the afterlife.
56 If you spent your life at parties, you would have a terrible time, assuming you managed to get there at all.
57 It is a funny idea so try the two who write comedies.
58 Top cat.
59 He was neither a Barchester nor a Palliser character.
60 Not one of his historical novels.
61 Think of one of his Oxford contemporaries.
62 She was a spirited lady.
63 Choose an African country.
64 Think of dates and work out their ages.
65 Eliminate the Glorious Twelfth and Hallowe'en.
66 Eliminate the Indian and Far Eastern traditions.
67 It doesn't look like an African name.
68 Polo and cricket, didgeridoos and little furry creatures leave no time for sailing.
69 Eliminate the hedonists and the doubters.

70 Choose either the one from India or from China.

71 Think of the two men who did designs for other museums.

72 French sounding names are misleading here.

73 It has neither biblical nor animal associations.

74 Ignore the rugby star and the potter.

75 Eliminate stammering and lack of co-ordination.

76 Choose one of the two writers much influenced by Existentialism.

77 Eliminate the composer of enigmas and the star-gazer.

78 This temple was in the capital of the ancient Khmer empire.

79 It is named neither after Mr Humphries nor his goat.

80 Go for one of the two who have theatres named after them.

81 America helped to found it for freed slaves.

82 See if you can work out a million to the fifth power.

83 Choose between fear and hunger.

84 Only two of these artists worked in the Sistine Chapel.

85 Remember Leander's connection with water.

86 Choose one of the two Imagist poets.

87 Sherrill could be a woman's name but here it is a man's.

88 Win with a blue.

89 Neither on the home of Odysseus nor Minos.

90 It has changed its name to Myanmar and borders old Siam.

91 Despite their collective name, they are not man-eaters.

92 Choose one of the Absurdist writers.

93 A trophy for a triumphant tourist.

94 Choose between two former neighbours in Twickenham.

95 He was not star-struck in any sense of the word.

96 Choose between a Long Island or a French Riviera setting.

97 He had nothing to do with textiles.

98 It was named after an American engineer who made geodesic domes.

99 This sect is neither in the mystic nor the mainstream tradition.

100 He didn't need balls for this.

101 He could either be French or American.

102 A layer in addition to the core.

103 Choose one of the female choreographers.

104 I am aware.

105 He was German not Austrian.

106 He made an effort to bear his cross with courage.

107 You get lumps not spots with this one.

108 Eliminate two cities once dominated by the Medici and the Visconti.

109 It was neither of the two sisters.

110 Think holistically and mythologically.

111 He carried the play.

112 They are neither North nor South Pacific islanders.

113 Choose between one who made this nectar into a bedtime drink for mortals or another who gave all plants a Latin name.

114 Eliminate the Austrian and the German Holy Roman Emperors.

115 Maybe the fall killed him.

116 Do republican Aussies still enjoy the sport of kings or do they prefer to burn the bails?

117 Choose between one or other of the Nobel laureates.

118 Surprisingly, it was neither of the directors of the RSC.

119 It probably doesn't want to be shot.

120 Say hello and maybe anything goes.

121 Ignore the tilter at windmills and the bullfighter.

122 Eliminate one that is sacred to present day Orthodox monks and another that was home to all the gods.

123 It was neither the 'Rule Britannia' nor the 'Land of Hope and Glory' man.

124 Choose one of two reluctant members of the European Union.

125 Pay no attention to the comedian and the chamber pot.

126 She was either a Stuart or a Plantagenet queen.

127 Eliminate the French revolutionaries and those briefly in power before the Bolsheviks.

128 Choose one of two TV newscasters.

129 Narrow it down to two nuclear scientists closely involved in the Manhattan Project.

130 Eliminate the god and the dwarf.

131 He was an Italian architect.

132 Claimed and settled by the British, it would most likely be named after a Briton.

133 Fuzzy Wuzzy had no hair and you don't often see a shellfish on a bicycle.

134 It made a great impression.

135 This choir is based in the capital.

136 The rain's in Spain and they wouldn't want to spoil their kit.

137 They could be a dynastic family or just humble craftsmen.

138 It was either the Macedonian or the Mongol.

139 He could either be the son of an artist or an artist in his own right.

140 Eliminate Wordsworth's and Jane Austen's houses.

141 The wets go to Westminster.

142 Eliminate the discoverers of a comet and the law of gravity.

143 It could have been a royal visit to a doctor's surgery or a day out on a farm.

144 Choose between Fate or the magic of the South Seas.

145 The Sahara might provide its habitat.

146 Agassi Junior inherited his dad's punchiness even if he went in for a different racket.

147 Albert and Peter were local boys.

148 If you go into the mountains you might encounter one or the other but not to eat.

149 Think geographically - the North was Yankee.

150 Eliminate the royalist soldier and the author of 'Marmion'.

151 He came from neither the land of the gypsies nor vampires.

152 If he had slipped, could he have escaped or was he to do it again with a man in a wheelbarrow?

153 It was either the father or the son.

154 Razors are for keeping things shaved whether it be beards or ideas.

155 Think of two who have represented Great Britain at the Venice Biennale.

156 It could have been a grain of sand or a speck of soot.

157 The date was 1876.

158 Think of a part of what used to be known as the Holy Land.

159 Narrow it down to the two who worked on the grandest scale.

160 He was neither English nor patient.

161 He was one of two who contributed to a daily newspaper.

162 Go for one of the history plays.

163 It was neither the tearful mortal nor Dionysus' mother.

164 It could be associated with either water or the night.

165 SW1 and W8 are the posher areas.

166 He was an American evangelist.

167 He would have used his hands more than his brains.

168 He was given these titles when he was married.

169 They could have come from the roof of the world or the land of the rising sun.

170 Think of World War I.

171 Time to brush up your French and make a deduction.

172 Think of the reign in which this war took place.

173 This ridiculous word is commonly reduced to three letters.

174 They were not particularly warlike and were native to a part of Europe.

175 They live in the forests of Borneo or Uganda.

176 The presence of Clark Gable in one production and Tony Curtis and Jack Lemmon in another narrows it down.

177 Choose between the sound of a sailor or a horticulturist.

178 Strength and weight won the day for the coppers.

179 Either way it is a pretty spooky head.

180 In the same poem comes the line, 'Footfalls echo in the memory/ Down the passage which we did not take/ Towards the door we never opened/ Into the rose-garden.'

181 Choose one of the World War I poets.

182 His subjects are either biters or wrigglers.

183 Choose a town which did not later become a bishopric.

184 The answer lies in the natural world.

185 It could be a city in Morocco or the Yemen.

186 Either she who launched a thousand ships or the serpent of the Nile.

187 Think of the Iberian coastline.

188 Was he drawn to this title by too much previous dolce vita or the fatal bite of a leopard?

189 Choose between the two most florid and ornate styles.

190 Proverbially one choice could be the victim of another early one.

191 Remember Shakespeare's play.

192 They enjoyed relaxing away from their offices.

193 It is the opposite to splitting or dividing.

194 He was a Plantagenet king.

195 Remembering your Latin, choose the one with the feminine ending.

196 He flew and swung with Ginger.

197 It is not the man who invented the C5 but he was one of the first computer nerds.

198 Geographically you would be unlikely to find them on Earth.

199 A rare exception to the Monroe Doctrine.

200 He plays for the same county as his brother-in-law.